African Economic Institutions

I0130677

This book analyzes how, and under what conditions, African international economic organizations (IEOs) have evolved, and what individual and collective contributions, if any, these African IEOs have made to Africa's socioeconomic development.

Providing a comprehensive and accessible overview, the book covers the continent's main IEOs: the United Nations Economic Commission on Africa, the African Development Bank, and the New Partnership for Africa's Development, as well as the five major regional economic communities (RECs), including the Economic Community of West African States, and the Southern African Development Community.

Assessing the degree to which African IEOs have been able to chart their own course in coming up with their development agendas and priorities rather than following the lead of global institutions, this book:

- provides a descriptive and analytical overview of the historical and contemporary development blueprints produced for Africa;
- clearly examines the contribution made by African economic institutions toward development;
- considers whether African economic institutions are building blocks or stumbling blocks in Africa's development;
- offers a detailed evaluation and critique of African IEOs.

Enabling the reader to reach a deeper understanding of the challenges and potentials of development on the African continent, *African Economic Institutions* will be of interest to all students and scholars of African politics and development studies.

Kwame Akonor is an Assistant Professor at Seton Hall University New Jersey, where he teaches International Relations, Comparative Politics and African Political Economy. He directs the university's Africana Center and is also Director of the African Development Institute, a New York-based think tank. He is the author of *Africa and IMF Conditionality* (Routledge, 2006).

Routledge Global Institutions

Edited by Thomas G. Weiss
The CUNY Graduate Center, New York, USA
and Rorden Wilkinson
University of Manchester, UK

About the Series

The "Global Institutions Series" is designed to provide readers with comprehensive, accessible, and informative guides to the history, structure, and activities of key international organizations. Every volume stands on its own as a thorough and insightful treatment of a particular topic, but the series as a whole contributes to a coherent and complementary portrait of the phenomenon of global institutions at the dawn of the millennium.

Books are written by recognized experts, conform to a similar structure, and cover a range of themes and debates common to the series. These areas of shared concern include the general purpose and rationale for organizations, developments over time, membership, structure, decision-making procedures, and key functions. Moreover, current debates are placed in historical perspective alongside informed analysis and critique. Each book also contains an annotated bibliography and guide to electronic information as well as any annexes appropriate to the subject matter at hand.

The volumes currently published include:

Books currently under contract include:

The UN Secretary-General and Secretariat, 2nd edition
by Leon Gordenker (Princeton University)

Governing Climate Change
by Peter Newell (University of East Anglia) and Harriet A. Bulkeley (Durham University)

Multilateral Counter-Terrorism
The global politics of cooperation and contestation
by Peter Romaniuk (John Jay College of Criminal Justice, CUNY)

Preventive Human Rights
Strategies in a world of acute threats and challenges
by Bertrand G. Ramcharan (Geneva Graduate Institute of International and Development Studies)

Non-Governmental Organizations in Global Politics
by Peter Willetts (City University, London)

The International Labour Organization
by Steve Hughes (University of Newcastle) and Nigel Haworth (University of Auckland Business School)

The Regional Development Banks
Lending with a regional flavor
by Jonathan R. Strand (University of Nevada)

Peacebuilding
From concept to commission
by Robert Jenkins (The CUNY Graduate Center)

Millennium Development Goals (MDGs)
For a people-centered development agenda?
by Sakiko Fukada-Parr (The New School)

Human Security
by Don Hubert (University of Ottawa)

Global Poverty
by David Hulme (University of Manchester)

UNESCO
by J. P. Singh (Georgetown University)

UNICEF
by Richard Jolly (University of Sussex)

The Organization of American States (OAS)
by Mônica Herz (Instituto de Relações Internacionais)

FIFA
by Alan Tomlinson (University of Brighton)

International Law, International Relations, and Global Governance
by Charlotte Ku (University of Illinois, College of Law)

Humanitarianism Contested
by Michael Barnett (University of Minnesota) and Thomas G. Weiss (The CUNY Graduate Center)

Forum on China-Africa Cooperation (FOCAC)
by Ian Taylor (University of St. Andrews)

The Bank for International Settlements
The politics of global financial supervision in the age of high finance
by Kevin Ozgercin (SUNY College at Old Westbury)

Global Health Governance
by Sophie Harman (City University, London)

International Migration
by Khalid Koser (Geneva Centre for Security Policy)

Think Tanks
by James McGann (University of Pennsylvania) and Mary Johnstone Louis (University of Oxford)

The Council of Europe
by Martyn Bond (The London Press Club)

The International Monetary Fund, 2nd edition
Politics of conditional lending
by James Raymond Vreeland (Georgetown University)

The United Nations Development Programme (UNDP)
by Stephen Browne (The International Trade Centre, Geneva)

For further information regarding the series, please contact:

Craig Fowlie, Senior Publisher, Politics & International Studies
Taylor & Francis
2 Park Square, Milton Park, Abingdon
Oxford OX14 4RN, UK

+44 (0)207 842 2057 Tel
+44 (0)207 842 2302 Fax

Craig.Fowlie@tandf.co.uk
www.routledge.com

African Economic Institutions

Kwame Akonor

Routledge
Taylor & Francis Group
LONDON AND NEW YORK

First published 2010
by Routledge
2 Park Square, Milton Park, Abingdon, Oxfordshire OX14 4RN

Simultaneously published in the USA and Canada
by Routledge
711 Third Avenue, New York, NY 10017

Routledge is an imprint of the Taylor & Francis Group, an informa business

First issued in paperback 2011

© 2009 Kwame Akonor

Typeset in Times New Roman by
Taylor & Francis Books

British Library Cataloguing in Publication Data
A catalogue record for this book is available from the British Library

Library of Congress Cataloging in Publication Data
Akonor, Kwame.
    African economic institutions / Kwame Akonor.
       p. cm. – (Global institutions)
    Includes bibliographical references and index.
    1. Institutional economics–History. 2. Africa–Economic conditions. 3.
    Africa–Economic policy. I. Title.
    HB99.5.A46 2009
    337.6–dc22   2009021128

ISBN13: 978-0-415-77637-0 (hbk)
ISBN13: 978-0-415-50045-6 (pbk)
ISBN13: 978-0-203-86521-7 (ebk)

Contents

Illustrations

Foreword

The current volume is the thirty-eighth in our ongoing series on "global institutions," which continues to grow but remains dynamic in every way. Since the first titles appeared in 2005, the series has strived to provide readers with definitive guides to the most visible aspects of what we know as "global governance." Remarkable as it may seem, there exist relatively few books that offer in-depth treatments of prominent global bodies, processes, and associated issues, much less an entire series of concise and complementary volumes. Those that do exist are either out of date, inaccessible to the non-specialist reader, or seek to develop a specialized understanding of particular aspects of an institution or process rather than offer an overall account of its functioning. Similarly, existing books have often been written in highly technical language or have been crafted "in-house" and are notoriously self-serving and narrow.

The advent of electronic media has helped by making information, documents, and resolutions of international organizations more widely available, but it has also complicated matters. The growing reliance on the internet and other electronic methods of finding information about key international organizations and processes has served, ironically, to limit the in-depth educational materials to which most readers have ready access—namely, books. Public relations documents, raw data, and loosely refereed web sites do not make for intelligent analysis. Official publications compete with a vast amount of electronically available information, much of which is suspect because of its ideological or self-promoting slant. Paradoxically, a growing range of purportedly independent web sites offering analyses of the activities of particular organizations emerged, but one inadvertent consequence has been to frustrate access to basic, authoritative, critical, and well researched texts. The market for such has actually been reduced by the ready availability of varying quality electronic materials.

For those of us who teach, research, and practice in the area, this access to information has been particularly frustrating. We were delighted when Routledge saw the value of a series that bucks this trend and provides key reference points to the most significant global institutions. They know that serious students and professionals want serious analyses. We have assembled a first-rate line-up of authors to address that need and that market. Our intention is to provide one-stop shopping for all readers—students (both undergraduate and postgraduate), negotiators, diplomats, practitioners from nongovernmental and intergovernmental organizations, and interested parties alike—seeking information about the most prominent institutional aspects of global governance.

African economic institutions

The economic and social performance of many of Africa's states since independence has been far from spectacular, even if it is an exaggeration to say, as travel writer and novelist Paul Theroux does, that "all news out of Africa is bad."[1] Clearly the news has not been pleasant from a continent that has witnessed massive displacement and war, dramatic falls in human wellbeing, growth in a small number of economic sectors and catastrophe in many more, and the accumulation of huge amounts of wealth by small elites and the relative and steady impoverishment of the many. But it is important not to ignore the advances that independent rule—however awkwardly realized—has brought to some parts of a continent that was until very recently still governed by European powers, and their settlers, in all-too-often brutal ways.

Much of the blame for Africa's less than spectacular performance has been attributed to the corruption and ethnic loyalties perceived to be endemic to the continent. And while it is the case that the legacies of colonialism and of inappropriate aid and trade regimes have also figured[2] (albeit to a much lesser extent) in explanations of the continent's underperformance, the institutions specifically charged with overseeing Africa's economic development have attracted almost no attention. Few scholars even note the existence of these bodies; while fewer still offer accounts of the role that they have played in the continuing underdevelopment of the continent.[3] This stands in stark contrast to the criticism that global economic institutions like the World Bank and International Monetary Fund have attracted for the role they have played in dealing with Africa's economic and social misfortunes.[4]

It is nevertheless the case that Africa's economic institutions—the United Nations Economic Commission for Africa (ECA), the African Development Bank (ADB), and the New Partnership for Africa's

Development (NEPAD)—have played a key role in Africa's development and its future prospects. They have acted as conduits for the imposition of global economic reforms that have brought many African states into line with neoliberal ideas about economic and political organization, while at the same time claiming to advance a distinctly African approach to the problems of underdevelopment. Yet, it is precisely because Africa's economic performance continues to be lackluster, and because the claims of these institutions all too often appear to ring hollow, that the role of these bodies needs to be brought to the fore. Moreover, it is precisely because there is a lack of understanding of their successes and failures as well as the politics and consequences of their actions that a coherent account of their activities is needed and is much overdue.

The relative inattention given to Africa's economic institutions, however, creates something of a problem; because few have considered exploring their role in Africa's development, few scholars are able to offer cogent accounts of their genesis, development, and activities. Kwame Akonor, however, is one of those few scholars. Kwame is an assistant professor of politics at Seton Hall University, whose teaching and research focus on international relations, law, and organization with a particular reference to Africa. An up-and-coming African political economist whose CUNY Graduate Center dissertation on IMF conditionality was also published by Routledge,[5] we are delighted to put his current work in front of our readers. As always, we look forward to comments from first-time or veteran readers of the Global Institutions series.

Thomas G. Weiss, the CUNY Graduate Center, New York, USA
Rorden Wilkinson, University of Manchester, UK
October 2009

Acknowledgments

The successful completion of this book would not have been possible had it not been for the steady support and encouragement from Thomas G. Weiss and Rorden Wilkinson, editors of this series. They provided extremely incisive feedback, but I am most grateful for their faith and patience as I worked on the project.

My experience at the Cambridge Advanced Programme on Rethinking Development Economics, under the leadership of Dr. Ha-Joon Chang, greatly refined my thinking in a lot of ways. Dr. LaDawn Haglund of Arizona State University deserves mention for the very useful comments that she provided, and which helped shape Chapter 3.

I dedicate this book to the memory of my mentor, great friend, and confidante, Dr. Ofuatey Kodjoe.

Finally, special thanks to the Akonor family, and to Monique, Efua Asantewaa, and Kwesi-Ansah Yeboa; they more than anyone know best what it took to write this book.

Abbreviations and acronyms

ACP	African, Caribbean, and Pacific
ADB	African Development Bank
APRM	Africa Peer Review Mechanism
AMU	Arab Maghreb Union
AU	African Union
BWI	Bretton Woods Institution
CEN-SAD	Community of Sahel-Saharan States
COMESA	Common Market for East and Southern Africa
EAC	East African Community
ECA	United Nations Economic Commission for Africa
ECCAS	Economic Community of Central African States
ECLA	United Nations Economic Commission for Latin America
ECOWAS	Economic Community of West African States
EEC	European Economic Community
EPA	Economic Partnership Agreement
EU	European Union
FDI	Foreign direct investment
GATT	General Agreement on Tariffs and Trade
GDP	Gross domestic product
GNP	Gross national product
HIPC	Highly indebted poor country
ILO	International Labour Organization
IMF	International Monetary Fund
ISI	Import-substituting industrialization
LPA	Lagos Plan of Action
MDG	Millennium Development Goal
NEPAD	New Economic Partnership for Africa's Development
NGO	Nongovernmental organization
OAU	Organization of African Unity

OECD	Organisation for Economic Co-operation and Development
PTA	Preferential Trade Area for Eastern and Southern African States
SACU	Southern African Customs Union
SADC	Southern African Development Community
SADCC	Southern African Development Coordination Conference
SAP	Structural adjustment program
SMEs	Small and medium-scale enterprises
SSA	Sub-Saharan Africa

Introduction

It has been half a century since most African countries gained independence to manage not only their political affairs but also their economic destinies. The results from the five decades of economic development have been anything but glowing. Occasionally, there has been modest macroeconomic stability and growth on the continent but they have been neither sustainable nor inclusive. The patterns of economic growth, when they have been positive, have not been sustainable because the overall structural foundations on which African economies rest are fragile and vulnerable to world commodity prices. Compounding this issue is the fact that Africa has a weak industrial base and a massive debt overhang. Similarly, any data celebrating development in Africa ought to be greeted with caution because such data have generally been uneven and mask the variation in economic performance among African countries. A recent case in point is this. The International Monetary Fund (IMF) in November 2008 forecasted that while economic growth will slow markedly for all regions in the coming year, Africa's economic performance will best other regions, with GDP projected at 5.2 percent in 2008 and 4.7 percent in 2009.[1] The uneven nature of such a forecast is aptly captured in the United Nations Conference on Trade and Development (UNCTAD)'s latest report on "least developed countries" (LDCs). Of the 50 countries designated by the UNCTAD as LDCs in 2008, more than half (33 countries to be precise) were in Africa.[2] One of the central claims of this book is that the crisis of development in Africa since independence is related to the policy choices and development models chosen by the actors responsible for the planning and executing of economic development, including African international economic organizations (IEOs).

IEOs and development

IEOs are created to foster trade and economic cooperation among their members, however, the unique and influential role that IEOs play in economic development affects members and non-members alike.[3] For example, the practical impact of the Bretton Woods Institutions (BWIs), the IMF and the World Bank, in promoting the recovery and reconstruction of Europe and Japan, immediately following World War II, is well documented.[4] The history of the European Economic Community (EEC) and its subsequent transformation into the European Union serves as an important reminder about the role of institutions in international relations in general, and regional policy implementation in particular.[5] Moreover, multilateral development banks play a key role in the development assistance strategies of their members by providing loans at concessional rates.

Beyond the provision of practical development assistance for their members, IEOs also provide important new ideas and intellectual arguments that may influence general development thinking. The fierce intellectual and policy critique in the early 1960s by the United Nations Economic Commission for Latin America (ECLA) to the modernization paradigm, which stressed that economic and social progress everywhere follows a linear trajectory, starting at a basic simplistic level and then evolving into a more complex systems level, is crucial to any nuanced understanding of the development challenges facing the global south.[6] The ECLA not only rejected the modernization thesis but it actively advocated an alternative development strategy, based on import substitution, which became the blueprint for many Latin American countries.[7]

In this regard, the mandate of African IEOs is no different from that of its regional and global counterparts: they exist to shape, influence, and assist with development policy of their members. The African IEOs that will be the central focus of this volume, The United Nations Economic Commission for Africa (ECA), The African Development Bank (ADB), and The New Partnership for Africa's Development (NEPAD) continue to play a crucial role in the development agenda of the continent. However, much of the diagnosis and policy prescriptions that the African IEOs favor are heavily determined by global IEOs, especially the World Bank and IMF. It is no wonder that African IEOs are generally supportive of the core neoliberal agenda. Commenting on this trend, Jeffery Sachs rightly noted that African countries, since independence,

> have looked to donor nations—often their former colonial rulers—and to the international financial institutions for guidance on growth. Indeed, since the onset of the African debt crisis of the

1980s, the guidance has become a kind of economic receivership, with the policies of many African nations decided in a seemingly endless cycle of meetings with the IMF and the World Bank, donors and creditors.[8]

The nearly universal emphasis by all the post-independence African development strategies on orthodox liberalism as formulaic prescriptions has led many scholars and activists to complain about the marginalization of African voices in the development debate.[9] For some, the development discourse has been a top-down, BWI-driven, elite process with African countries (and by extension African IEOs, the continent's primary economic policymaking bodies) playing a mere supportive and dormant role.[10] The critique is especially poignant since most development indicators show Africa as the region that has made the least progress at the beginning of the twenty-first century. If this is the case, the argument can be made that the historically close working relationship on economic policy issues between African IEOs and their global counterparts, and the excessive faith placed in neoliberal policies, make African IEOs indirect agents to the consolidation of Africa's underdevelopment and dependency. If on the other hand, African IEOs have been active and autonomous in advancing their own alternative development paradigms and policies, then a detailed analysis on the individual and collective (heterodox) African IEO contributions is warranted.

Though there is extensive literature on the role of the World Bank and IMF in Africa's development, any investigation of the role and impact of African IEOs as agents in the continent's development policymaking has received little scrutiny. This book, the first comparative study of the history and effectiveness of African IEOs, will therefore fill the gap in analysis by providing timely information on the role these institutions have played in Africa's development.

There are numerous economic institutions dealing with Africa, making it onerous for the researcher to provide a strict classification. For the purposes of this study, the African IEOs were chosen based on the fact that they are headquartered in Africa and their membership and scope of jurisdiction is continent-wide. According to S. A. Akintan, an African economic institution may be classified as continent-wide, as opposed to regional or local, if the membership is open to countries from the "whole continent of Africa, Madagascar, and other African islands."[11] Beneath this general classification lie several important differences. The ECA is an all-purpose, or general economic institution, while the ADB is a specialized financial economic institution. NEPAD, on the other hand, is a special case. Because it has no legal status in its own right (it is not a treaty, convention or charter with binding obligations) it can only be considered a quasi economic institution.

Notwithstanding the emphasis on these three continent-wide IEOs, significant attention will also be given to African regional economic communities (RECs). African RECs, such as the Economic Community of West African States (ECOWAS), have been, and remain, central institutional actors in Africa's efforts to resolve its economic development dilemmas. Indeed, Africa's political leaders see RECs as the pillars or building blocks for an African Economic Community (AEC), in which economic, fiscal, monetary, social and sectoral policies would be harmonized across the continent. The commitment to the eventual merger of RECs, and the creation of AEC, is enshrined in the 1991 Abuja Treaty, which lays down a 34-year timetable (1994–2028), in six different stages of different duration for the integration scheme (see Box I.1). Moreover, most RECs in Africa have undergone institutional reforms in response to changes in the global and regional political landscape, such as the demise of the Cold War and the end of apartheid. The presence and/or expansion of RECs pose somewhat of a conundrum for development analysts. For some, continent-wide IEOs and RECs are contradictory process whilst others view both institutions as mutually reinforcing. Still others see multiplicity and overlapping memberships in African RECs as barriers to member states' commitment to treaty compliance and policy implementation. (For a list of the locations of all the African IEOs, including RECs, see Map I.1).

Box I.1 Phases and goals of the African Economic Community

- First phase, 1994–99. Strengthen regional economic communities and establish them where they do not exist.
- Second phase, 1999–2007. Freeze tariffs, nontariff barriers, customs duties, and internal taxes at their May 1994 levels and gradually harmonize policies and implement multinational program in all economic sectors—particularly agriculture, industry, transport, communications, and energy.
- Third phase, 2007–17. Consolidate free trade zones and customs unions through progressive elimination of tariffs, nontariff barriers, and other restrictions to trade, and adopting common external tariffs.

(*Box continued on next page*)

- Fourth phase, 2017–19. Finalize coordination and harmonization of policies and programs in trade and other sectors as a precursor to full realization of the African Common Market and African Economic Community, with all regional economic communities. This phase should result in the free movement of people, with rights of residence and establishment among the regional economic communities.
- Fifth phase, 2019–23. Consolidate the continent-wide African Common Market resulting from the fourth phase.
- Sixth phase, 2023–28. Realize the vision of the African Economic Community, with complete economic, political, social, and cultural integration and with common structures, facilities, and functions, including a single African central bank, a single African currency, a pan-African parliament, and a pan-African economic and monetary union.

Source: The African Economic Community Treaty, 1991.

So in its overall contribution to the literature on global institutions, this volume seeks to find out why certain institutions perform better, or are more effective, than others in Africa. Toward that end, particular attention will be paid to three issues in the African context: capacity, autonomy, and accountability. Do African IEOs have the capacity to carry out their own growth-oriented projects or are they hampered and/or hijacked by an accumulating class, financial constraints, and ineffective bureaucracies? Do African IEOs have the autonomy to set agendas, shape policy, and provide, produce, and/or control information despite the fact that they, like all IEOs, are a collection of national government representatives sensitive to the realities of the prevailing political economy?[12] And finally, to what extent have African IEOs been agents of accountability to the overall societal needs that flow from their mandate, and how have they created opportunities for inclusiveness and participation of the broader publics, to whom their policies affect directly?

Structure of the book

The initial chapter will provide a brief description of the history, mission and development of each African IEO. Significant transitions in

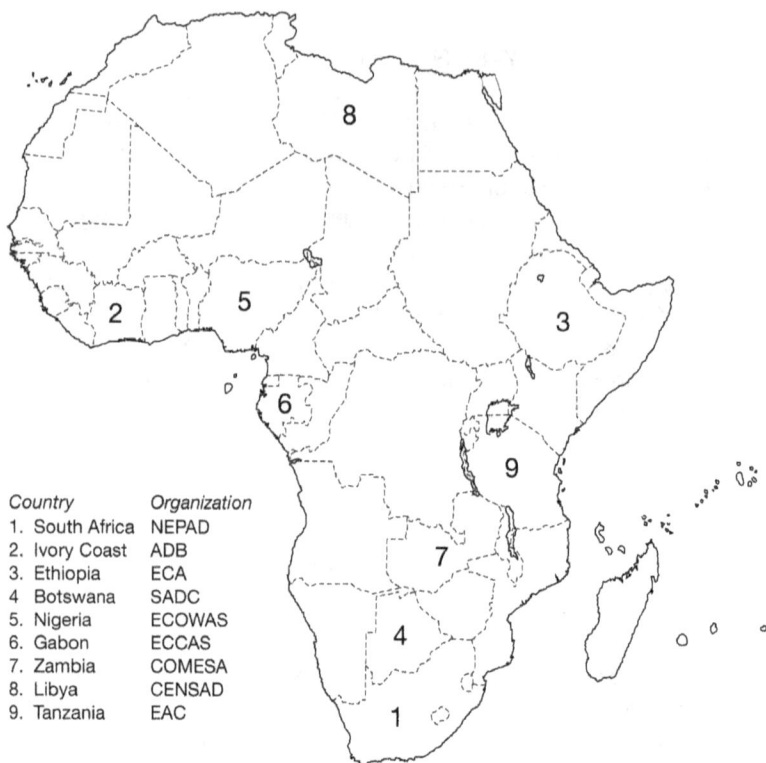

Country	Organization
1. South Africa	NEPAD
2. Ivory Coast	ADB
3. Ethiopia	ECA
4 Botswana	SADC
5. Nigeria	ECOWAS
6. Gabon	ECCAS
7. Zambia	COMESA
8. Libya	CENSAD
9. Tanzania	EAC

Map I.1 Location of African economic institutions

leadership as well as evolutions in each organization's philosophy of economic development will be also be analyzed, paying particular attention to the underlying dynamics and context of any such change. A part of this section will deal with how politics has affected African IEOs. For instance, the interaction and role that the Organization of African Unity (OAU)—now the African Union (AU)—and global institutions (BWIs in particular) have played in the development of each of these organizations will be examined. Some central questions in this chapter are: Have the purposes of ECA, ADB, and NEPAD changed, and if so, why and what is different now? What is the source of the economic philosophy of each African IEO? To what degree have African IEOs been able to chart their own course in coming up with their development agendas and priorities, and to what degree have they been pressured to follow the lead of the global institutions (such as the World Bank)?

Chapter 2 describes the structure and day-to-day functioning of ECA, ADB, and NEPAD. Each organization's "nuts and bolts" are discussed: membership, organizational structure, geographical locations, general activities, administrative capacity, including leadership, finances, and affiliated organs, are covered.

Chapter 3 is an appraisal and critique of each organization's role in African development policy. Some key questions which will be addressed are: What specific policy proposals are advocated by African IEOs and have they been successful in getting national policymakers to adopt them? Have they been effective in carrying out their tasks as development agents; and given the political economy within which they have to operate what factors are likely to make a difference their record of performance? This chapter concludes by noting the key criticisms of (and providing policy recommendations for) each organization.

Chapter 4 focuses on the main sub-regional organizations in Africa: Southern African Development Community (SADC), Economic Community of West African States (ECOWAS), East African Community (EAC), Economic Community of Central African States (ECCAS), Common Market for Eastern and Southern Africa (COMESA), and the Community of Sahel-Saharan States (CEN-SAD). The Arab Maghreb Union, which is considered one of the REC pillars of the envisioned AEC, is omitted from this study because it is virtually moribund. After a brief history and summary of the major activities of each REC, the chapter assesses their effectiveness and discusses the extent to which these sub-regional organizations pose challenges and/or solutions to the principal African IEOs discussed in this volume. Some of the lines of inquiry include: What role did African RECs in play in the pre/postcolonial era and what is the current state of their integration? To what extent are African RECs implemented effectively? How closely does their mission approximate to their practical results? Who are the key actors that drive African RECs, are they political or private (business) actors? Do African RECs substitute or complement national and local policy objectives? What consequences or impact do African RECs have on the development of African IEOs?

The concluding chapter examines how current events and changing perspectives might impact the effectiveness of each IEO. Transformative trends in African development today such as brain drain, globalization, the HIV/AIDS crisis, and China–Africa trade are discussed and analyzed. Will African IEOs and African RECs matter in the future of Africa's development, given current and future trends, and if so, how?

For the people of Africa, the success of these organizations is of the utmost importance. The pressing nature of the many economic issues facing Africans requires cooperation and creativity, and real progress must be made to improve the lot of the common citizen. However, these institutions must not simply give in to the conventional economic wisdom that may be more appropriate for industrialized nations. Neo-liberalism has had a poor record in Africa, and the cookie-cutter approach of the BWIs will undoubtedly benefit the international economic elites more than ordinary Africans. African IEOs must find their African voice, and remain steadfast in their role as advocates for their citizens. This implies a need to shift away from the dominant development policy paradigm toward a development framework that embraces pluralism. Without the unique perspective offered by African policymakers and leaders, these institutions will be of little use to those they seek to help.

1 The history of African economic institutions and their development agenda

One of the main motivations behind the creation of the ECA, the ADB and NEPAD was a desire by African policymakers to have economic autonomy when it comes to managing the affairs of the continent. The following pages recount the challenges and historical record of Africa's economic institutions. More importantly, the chapter seeks to find out if the economic independence that African IEOs so fiercely exhibited has in any way been compromised or weakened with time.

ECA

The question of establishing a regional economic commission for Africa was brought up as early as the ninth session of ECOSOC. On 11 March 1947 the delegation from India introduced a resolution calling for the establishment of a special economic commission for North Africa and Ethiopia. The Indian delegation felt that the creation of such an African commission was imperative since ECOSOC had earlier approved the establishment of the Economic Commission for Europe and an Economic Commission for Asia and the Far East. ECOSOC did not take any action on the proposal, and refused to do so again at its sessions in 1950 and 1951. ECOSOC objected to an Economic Commission for Africa then because it "thought that the establishment of such a commission would be premature, as it could be established only with the agreements of the principal governments in the area and the representatives of the governments administering the territories in Africa were not in favor of such action."[1]

The idea to establish the ECA did not feature on ECOSOC's agenda till Ghana gained its independence from Britain in March 1957. Frederick S. Arkhurst, the Deputy Permanent Representative of Ghana to the United Nations during this period, who served as *Chargé d'Affaires*, recalled how little time the Ghanaian delegation had to prepare for the

12th regular session of the UN General Assembly, scheduled for 15 September 1957.[2] Arkhurst notes that the Ghanaian delegation was consumed with the idea of ECA and felt that there was "a great possibility of mobilizing a solid constituency of Afro-Asian, Latin American, Scandinavian and a few other delegations to support a resolution in the Second Economic Committee and in the General Assembly, to request the ECOSOC to establish a Regional Economic Commission for Africa. Accordingly, the African delegations met regularly to develop a strategy to achieve this end."[3]

Together with their Asian and Latin American counterparts, the African delegation agreed on a resolution for ECOSOC, which recommended "for the purpose of giving effective aid to the countries and territories of Africa, the Economic and Social Council should give prompt and favorable consideration to the establishment of an Economic Commission for Africa."[4] The initial sponsors of the resolution were: Afghanistan, Brazil, Burma, Cambodia, Ceylon, Chile, Egypt, Ethiopia, Ghana, Haiti, India, Indonesia, Iran, Iraq, Lebanon, Liberia, Libya, Mexico, Morocco, Nepal, Pakistan, Philippines, Poland, Saudi Arabia, Sudan, Syria, Tunisia, Yemen, and Yugoslavia.

According to Arkhurst, when the resolution was circulated to members of the Second Economic Committee, the delegations of the colonial powers, comprising of Belgium, Britain, France, Portugal and Spain, "reacted with great consternation." The British and the Belgians in particular tried to get the Ghanaian delegation to withdraw the resolution, arguing "that Africa did not really need an economic commission; that, in any case, the colonial powers were always available to support Africa with economic development assistance."[5] The Ghanaian delegation did not budge and countered that if Europe, one of the most economically advanced regions of the world, deserved and had its own regional economic commission, then so did Africa.

The colonial powers continued to question the wisdom of an ECA institution. This time they used the Committee for Technical Cooperation in Africa South of the Sahara (CCTA), which was established in 1950 by the colonial powers "to maintain links between them and their former colonies after independence, and to promote mutual economic cooperation." The supporters of CCTA felt a need for an African forum since the UN at the time had little interest in Africa. Although CCTA was created to deal in technical matters, critics, including Ambassador Arkhurst, claimed that the CCTA was political ploy by the colonial powers to keep the UN out, to reduce the publicity given to African problems, and to "maintain their control of their African colonies."[6] Ghana, which by this time was the only African member of the CCTA in the UN, was again persuaded by the CCTA representatives of Belgium, Britain, France, Portugal and Spain to withdraw the resolution. They tried to impress on the Ghanaian delegation that "Africa was really two entities—North Africa and Africa south of the Sahara—and that the two entities had different problems and objectives which could not be accommodated under the same Economic Commission."[7] Again, the Ghanaian delegation was not moved and formally submitted the ECA proposal for debate on 21 October 1957. At the end of the debate the Second Economic Committee overwhelmingly adopted the resolution on 24 October 1957, by a vote of 70 in favor, and none against (with Belgium and the United Kingdom abstaining). The General Assembly of the United Nations, on 26 November 1957, unanimously adopted the resolution, again with Belgium abstaining.

The ECA was established in 29 April 1958 under resolution 67aA (XXV) of the Economic and Social Council of the United Nations (ECOSOC). It was one of the four regional commissions created by ECOSOC by virtue of its powers contained in Article 68(2) of the United Nations Charter.[8] There are currently five such regional commissions.

Membership changes and mandate

Membership in early regional commissions was not exclusive to countries of a particular region. Not surprisingly, the ECA's membership at the time of its founding in 1958 was more colonial than African, but this changed shortly after the 1960s when a majority of African states gained independence. The 1958 document specifying the ECA's terms of reference states in paragraph 5: "Membership of the Commission shall be open to Belgium, Ethiopia, France, Ghana, Italy, Liberia, Morocco, Portugal, Spain, Sudan, Tunisia, the Union of South Africa, the United Arab Republic, and the United Kingdom of Great Britain and Northern Ireland, and to any state in the area which may hereafter become a Member of the United Nations, provided the States which shall cease to have any territorial responsibilities in Africa shall cease to be members of the commission." Paragraph 6 in the terms of reference states that, for the territories in Africa under colonial rule, they could apply to be a part of the ECA only if the states governing them presented their application to the commission. Upon acceptance, they would become associate members of the commission—not full members. The associate members at the birth of the ECA were: the Federation of Nigeria, Gambia, Kenya and Zanzibar, Sierra Leone, Somaliland Protectorate, Tanganyika, and Uganda. Once a territory became independent, then it could apply directly for membership through the Commission and it would be a full member.[9]

As more African states became independent they put pressure on the UN General Assembly to change the ECA membership requirements. Resolution 1466 was subsequently adopted in 1959, requesting that member states of the ECA propose the participation of colonial territories.[10] As a result, associate member states that were not yet independent were admitted to the ECA, including Burundi and Rwanda. From 1960 onward, more territories in Africa gained independence, and by virtue of belonging to the UN, they became a part of the ECA. So the character of the ECA became increasingly African, which prompted a review of the membership of colonial powers in the ECA. The bone of contention was compliance of colonial powers with UN resolution 1466. Portugal and Spain were targeted for not complying, and South Africa was targeted for its apartheid government. Eventually, ECOSOC, in 1963, expelled Portugal from the ECA for noncompliance with resolution 1466 (Spain had already complied at that point) and reworked the ECA's original terms of reference to downgrade the colonial powers to associate member status, which meant that African members would have the primary say in the ECA. Non-governing territories were still relegated to associate membership. ECOSOC allowed South Africa to remain a member of the ECA, but forbade it to participate in the Commission until it changed its racial policy.[11]

The Ethiopia-based ECA was mandated to promote the economic and social development of its member states, foster intra-regional integration, and promote international cooperation for Africa's development. The legal framework, which is referred to in resolution 67aA (XXV) above as "the terms of reference of the Economic Commission for Africa," provides that the ECA, like the other UN regional commissions, operate with a dual mandate: it is required to act "within the framework of the policies of the United Nations and subject to the general supervision of the Economic and Social Council" and at the same time serve its constituents, the African states (whose sovereign powers must be respected at all times). Thus, the ECA can only take action if it has the consent of the African member states, and where its policy advice is likely to significantly impact the global economy, it must submit such proposals to ECOSOC for consideration. Furthermore, the ECA must seek the approval of the ECOSOC before establishing any subordinate organs.

The ECA, which held its first session in Addis Ababa, Ethiopia, on 28 December 1958 through 6 January 1959, was given a number of tasks to assist African nations. The first of these was arranging for exchange of knowledge and experience of common problems at a technical level by means of conferences, meetings and seminars attended by experts from African countries and supported by consultations from African and non-African countries, and by arranging meetings between African leaders for the formulation of policy recommendations to governments or for negotiating multinational economic arrangements or the establishment of common institutions. Additionally, the organization was charged with increasing the opportunities for the training of African national supervisory or executive personnel through short intensive training centers and institutes. The ECA was also required to provide, through the regional advisory service and in other ways, on-the-spot assistance to the governments in development planning, public administration, trade promotion, natural resources, and development. Finally, the ECA was responsible for collecting, collating and disseminating statistical information, and the conducting and publishing of economic surveys and analytical studies.[12] Thus, the ECA was set up like a development think tank: formulating development strategies and making recommendations for its implementation, coordinating decision makers via meetings and seminars, advising governments and sub-regional organizations, performing research and policy analysis, disseminating reports and documents, and providing training and overseeing projects.

The ECA terms of reference were, however, unique in that they were drafted by Africans for Africans, and the scope of the Commission's work was expanded to include the social aspects of economic development.[13] The Commission was empowered, inter alia, to:

- Initiate and participate in measures for facilitating concerted action for the economic development of Africa, including its social aspects;
- Assist in the formulation and development of coordinated policies as a basis for practical action in promoting economic and technological development in the region;
- In carrying out the above functions, deal as appropriate with the social aspects of economic development and the inter-relationship of economic and social factors;
- After discussion with any specialized agency concerned and with the approval of the Economic and Social Council, establish such subsidiary bodies as it deemed appropriate for facilitating the carrying out of its responsibilities.

The ECA's uniqueness both in terms of spirit and scope is particularly salient when we consider the ECA's discourse on development, which will be discussed later in this chapter.

The African Development Bank (ADB)

The end of colonialism and the advent of new African leaders inspired several proposals in the late 1950s and early 1960s on how to finance the continent's vast development projects.[14] However, it was the vision of consolidating the fragmented continent of Africa in antithesis to the colonial powers, and the leadership provided by the ECA, that culminated in the establishment of the ADB. The ECA at its third session in February 1961 adopted resolution 27 (III) requesting its executive secretary to look into the feasibility of establishing a development bank for Africa. The executive secretary set a panel of experts to study the concept. The panel's "Report on the Possibility of Establishing an African Development Bank," which called for the speedy establishment of the ADB, was unanimously adopted at the ECA's fourth session, held in Addis Ababa from February to March 1962, by its resolution 52 (IV).[15] This same resolution created a committee of nine countries (Cameroon, Ethiopia, Guinea, Liberia, Mali, Nigeria, Sudan, Tanganyika (now part of Tanzania) and Tunisia), and charged it with the task of further research and consultations on the creation of the ADB. The committee met three times: in Monrovia (Liberia) from 18 to 22 June 1962, in Douala (Cameroon) from 24 to 27 September 1962, and in Casablanca (Morocco) from 14 to 23 January 1963. The outcome of these sessions was an ADB Draft Agreement, which was subsequently approved by the conference of finance ministers and African governments on 4 August 1963. The treaty establishing the ABD entered into force on 10 September 1964, and on 4 November 1964, the first board of governors meeting was held in Lagos, Nigeria. Mamoun Beheiry of Sudan was elected the first president of the ADB, and operations started on 1 July 1966, in Abidjan, Ivory Coast, with a staff of ten and $250 million in initial capital. Though it is permanently headquartered in Côte d'Ivoire, the ADB was temporarily relocated to Tunisia in 2003 for security reasons.

Membership and organizational changes

The goal of the ADB is to promote economic and social development through loans, equity investments, and technical assistance to its members. It is also dedicated to promoting development-related investment of public and private capital, responding to members' requests to help coordinate development policies and plans, and focusing on national and multinational projects and programs promoting regional integration. The entire organization is called the ADB Group, and it has three components: the African Development Fund (ADF), the

Nigeria Trust Fund (NTF), and the African Development Bank. The founders of the ADB intended it to be a wholly African institution, which meant it did not want any non-regional members included. In practice, however, the exclusion of non-regional members was not very practical; it ended up hampering the initial efforts of the Bank because its African members did not have much to contribute in terms of funding or expertise. As a result of these operational and financial difficulties, the ADB was relatively unknown, both within and outside of Africa. The ADB realized over time that it could not fulfill its goals—or even cover the basics of operations—without allowing non-regional members to join. In 1982, an amendment to the ADB's charter was finally tacked on, permitting the admission of non-African members to the Bank. However, in order to prevent the Bank from losing its African character, certain stipulations were made: the ADB's headquarters must remain in Africa and the Bank's president must be African; non-African member voting power and presence was limited to one-third of the board; and only African members could deal in loan operations and would hold two-thirds of the share capital.[16] Interviewed by a *Jeune Afrique* reporter about whether the ADB was suffering from an identity crisis due to the increasing number of non-African members, Omar Kabbaj, the ADB president from August 1995 to September 2005, responded: "remember that I am also an African and that I am sensitive to African realities. What is Africanity? Those who ask the question (whether the Bank is losing its African character)—and I am going to be very candid—obviously have a longing for the old Bank that was unproductive, unprofessional, disorganized ... To me Africanity means excellence, rigor, professionalism."[17] Currently, the ADB's shareholders include 53 African countries and 24 non-African countries from the Americas, Asia, and Europe.

Even after this amendment was put in place, the ADB still had to contend with political infighting that hobbled its effectiveness. Part of the reason for the weakness had to do with the office of the president. The managerial structure of the ADB until 1995 was such that the president did not really have executive authority over the Bank's operations in practice. The president was often overshadowed by the board of directors and even his own vice-presidents, who were supposed to be under his authority but who felt more beholden to the directors. The ensuing climate of anarchy and the highly politicized governance brought ADB close to complete collapse. Indeed, the wide ranging management and financial problems caused the ADB, on 30 August 1995, to lose its AAA credit rating, the only IEO to do so, just four days after a new bank president was elected.

The fact is, that prior to its 25th anniversary (1989), the ADB had received little to no scrutiny, but that all began to change when rumors of the Bank's ineffectiveness gradually began to surface. The first notable independent analysis of the ADB, though neutral, was Karen Mingst's *Politics of the African Development Bank* (1990). That same year, Bo Jerlstrom published *Banking on Africa: An Evaluation of the African Development Bank*. His criticism emphasized the fact that the ADB was trying "to be all things to all men." He recommended a long-term restructuring exercise that would have the ADB focus only on a few priorities. His conclusion: "Less African politics and a more professional banking approach would achieve greater development impact." In 1991, the Danish aid agency, DANIDA, also commissioned a study of the field effectiveness of eleven multilateral agencies in four countries, including Kenya and Sudan, where the role of the ADB Group was assessed. The study team, in its review of ADB operations, felt that it had tried to do too many things too quickly and that a refocus of its mission was in order. Perhaps the hardest hitting critique was the 1994 report of the ADB Task Force on Project Quality entitled "The Quest for Quality," often referred to as the Knox Report after the task force chairman, David Knox. The report, which was widely circulated, pointed to the need for a new management climate. The Knox Report advised that for the ADB to survive it will have to "instill a new culture, which will include fundamental changes in personnel management and in governance ... The Bank must be transparent, everyone accountable. Delegation and responsibility must be encouraged, objectively ensured by effective controls and information systems ... The president must be given the authority to lead the board and manage the Bank."[18]

Following the downgrading of the Bank's credit rating by Standard and Poor's in August 1995, *Euromoney*, a preeminent world finance publication, called the Bank an "international embarrassment," saying it was "hopelessly inefficient and shoddily managed."[19] The *Economist* said the Bank was "an inefficient, corrupt and politicized shambles."[20] The board of governors finally decided to step in. A committee was appointed in 1995 to analyze the situation and come up with recommendations. These recommendations suggested that directors should not serve for more than two terms and that the president must have practical authority as a CEO who sets strategy and appoints vice-presidents. The VPs could not become president until they resigned and applied at least two years later. The committee also recommended that the Bank establish standards on par with similar institutions. Emboldened by the new management changes, the newly elected president, Omar Kabbaj, began a 10-year restructuring aimed at restoring the Bank's financial health. Under Kabbaj's leadership there was centralization of operations, downsizing of staff (at least 300 employees were affected), and the closing of all regional offices. The results led to the restoration of the Bank's AAA credit rating and the recovery of shareholder confidence in the Bank's financial integrity. The Bank's formally shrinking lending portfolio was again on the upswing.

The New Partnership for Africa's Development (NEPAD)

The New Partnership for Africa's Development (NEPAD) seeks to eliminate poverty and support the progress of sustainable development in Africa, to maximize Africa's integration in the global economy, and to promote gender equality and empowerment. As the twenty-first century approached, and with the continent rid of colonialism and vestiges of the Cold War, African leaders decided to create two institutions to tackle the continent's development conundrum. A new political continental body, the African Union (AU), was created to replace the Organization of African Unity (OAU), and a new economic institution, NEPAD, was created. The story of NEPAD can be traced to the 4th OAU extraordinary summit held in Sirte, Libya during September 1999. This extraordinary summit was a result of an invitation extended by the Libyan leader, Col. Muammar Al Qathafi, at the 35th OAU summit in July 1999 in Algiers, for African leaders to "strengthen OAU capacity to enable it to meet the challenges of the new millennium." The summit charged President Thabo Mbeki of South Africa and President Abdelaziz Bouteflika of Algeria to press Africa's creditors for the total cancellation of Africa's external debt.[21] Following this, President Mbeki and President Olusegun Obasanjo of Nigeria were urged by the south summit of the Non-Aligned Movement (NAM), and the G-77, held in Havana, Cuba during April 2000, to take similar concerns of the South to the G-8 and the BWIs.[22]

With an eye toward an equal and constructive partnership with the North, the OAU at its summit held in Togo in July 2000 mandated that the three presidents raise the issue of engagement and partnership with the leaders of the G-8 at their summit in Japan during July 2000.[23] It is against this backdrop that the three presidents—of Algeria in its capacity as chair of the OAU, South Africa in its capacity as chair of the NAM, and Nigeria in its capacity as the chair of the Group-of-77 within the UN—launched the Millennium Partnership for the African Recovery Program (MAP). The MAP issued a call for a partnership between Africa and the rest of the world, specifically the industrial countries, to assist in achieving an African recovery, and identified five interdependent priority objectives, to be implemented simultaneously: The establishment of peace, security and good governance; investment in Africa's people; the diversification of Africa's production and exports; investment in information and communication technologies (ICT) and other basic infrastructure; and, the development of financing mechanisms to meet the present challenges.

Contemporaneously, another development initiative for the continent, the OMEGA Plan, was conceived by President Abdoulaye Wade of Senegal and was first presented at the Franco-Africa Summit in Yaoundé, Cameroon in January 2001. The OMEGA Plan was premised on four central pillars: building of infrastructures, including the new technologies of information and communication (ICT); education and human resource development; health; and agriculture. (It is reported that the three presidents who conceived MAP became aware of the Omega Plan for the first time at the World Economic Forum in Davos, Switzerland, on 30 January 2001. This suggests that the MAP was not sufficiently discussed amongst African leaders.)

During the 5th extraordinary summit of the OAU, again held in Sirte, Libya from March 2001, the various initiatives for the regeneration of the continent were floated and discussed. President Obasanjo made a presentation on MAP and President Wade of Senegal presented the OMEGA Plan. The summit endorsed both initiatives and suggested that all the continental initiatives, including the ECA's New Global Compact with Africa, be integrated into one foundational development document.[24] The task of creating this document was given to the heads of state of Algeria, Egypt, Nigeria, Senegal, and South Africa. The various initiatives were merged, and on 11 July 2001, NEPAD (or the New African Initiative, NAI, as it was temporarily known at the time), was presented to the OAU summit in Lusaka, Zambia. NEPAD was unanimously adopted in the form of Declaration 1 (XXXVII) as "Africa's principal agenda for development, providing a holistic, comprehensive integrated strategic framework for the socio-economic development of the continent, within the institutional framework of the African Union." The leaders of the G-8 countries subsequently endorsed NEPAD on 20 July 2001 in Genoa, Italy. In October 2001, African leaders met in Abuja, Nigeria and formally launched NEPAD.

Membership and guiding principles

As a program of the AU, NEPAD's membership comprises the African heads of state, and is guided by a wide range of principles and objectives.

- Ensuring African ownership, responsibility and leadership.
- Making Africa attractive to both domestic and foreign investors.
- Unleashing the vast economic potential of the continent.
- Achieving and sustaining an average gross domestic product (GDP) growth rate of over 7 percent per annum for the next 15 years.
- Ensuring that the continent achieves the agreed International Development Goals (IDGs).
- Increasing investment in human resource development.
- Promoting the role of women in all activities.
- Promoting sub-regional and continental economic integration.
- Developing a new partnership with industrialized countries and multilateral organizations on the basis of mutual commitments, obligations, interest, contributions and benefits.
- Strengthening Africa's capacity to lead her own development and to improve coordination with development partners.
- Ensuring that there is a capacity to lead negotiations on behalf of the continent on major development programs that require coordination at a continental level.
- Ensuring that there is capacity to accelerate implementation of major regional development cooperation agreements and projects already approved or in the pipeline.
- Strengthening Africa's capacity to mobilize additional external resources for its development.

NEPAD is thus programmatically structured to address three broad issues: the preconditions for sustainable development, policy reforms and increased investment in priority sectors, and mobilization of resources.

A quick summary of these African IEOs has indicated that while all institutions have a continent-wide development focus, each has a unique attribute as it relates to their implementation capacity. As the oldest African IEO, the ECA has played a crucial role in the establishment of both the ADB and the NEPAD. However, it appears constrained by the politics of the UN system that founded it and the lack of vision that has characterized most of Africa's leaders (more on this in the next section). On the other hand, the ADB, as the premier continental bank, has more implementation capacity, and hence more potential power, than the other African IEOs. However, the ADB too appears to be handicapped for a host of reasons. Chief amongst these is that it is having a hard time serving the African continent as an autonomous body without compromising its relationship with the more powerful IEOs. The newest arrival, NEPAD, is interesting in that it is the only African IEO that was created with a specific socio-economic development blueprint or paradigm in mind.

A shift toward neoliberalism

As the historical development of the African IEOs shows, there was an initial desire to maintain a certain level of independence when it came to economic policy. The ECA was successful in getting a social component added to its economic mandate, and the ADB was wary of admitting non-African members. But somehow the reliance on economic self-sufficiency gave way to dependence in economic thinking. NEPAD, though, is a different proposition as it is more of a manifestation of the capitulation driven by ECA and ABD. In what follows we will trace how the African IEOs lost their independence.

The story of the shift in emphasis from a state-led industrialization strategy through import substitution, amongst the many alternatives in development economics and practice, to one of "monoeconomics" where the neoliberal focus on market efficiency and a non-interventionist developmental state have become the only framework for analyzing economic problems, and perforce solutions, is best told through the economic history of postcolonial Africa.[25] The fact that Africa experienced decent levels of growth in the decade following independence based on the (now much maligned) import-substitution industrialization, is by itself not especially interesting.[26] After all, as Collier and Gunning and others remind us, the growth during this period did not rest on any solid foundation and was excessively vulnerable to external shocks.[27] The general consensus is that, "the external environment of the 1960–75 period favored an accumulation process that was based on import substitution mainly financed by earnings from exports of primary products. Impressive though the rates of growth of many African countries were, the economies remained highly vulnerable."[28] What is more significant is that African countries during this period had greater freedom over their macroeconomic and development policies than at any other period after their independence. Unfortunately, the framework of pluralism in general economic thinking, which in turn created an enhanced policy space for African policymakers, died shortly after the oil crisis of the mid-1970s. Since then, neoliberalism has been touted, especially by BWIs, not as one of the many "microfoundations to macroeconomics" but as the only model for economic management and development. Though the development results under this model for Africa have been abysmal,[29] African IEOs, rather than regaining an independent path in policymaking, seem to have surrendered their autonomy to the BWIs. In 1978, for example, only two African countries followed IMF-inspired policies. By 1990, this number had jumped to 28.[30] This is not to suggest that the African IEOs have done nothing. Rather, it is the uncreative mindset that the African IEOs are trapped in, and their inability to come up with serious economic solutions, that remains problematic. This change in orientation can be seen in all three of the IEOs examined here, and each gives an illustration of the power that the new neoliberal agenda has had in Africa.

The ECA and Africa's development discourse

As Africa's economic crisis accelerated, especially in the mid-to-late 1970s, the ECA at the urging of the United Nations General Assembly (and together with the other regional economic commissions) undertook an audit of the long-term development trends on the continent covering the period 1960 to 1975. The study revealed that Africa was the worst economic performer of all the regions, and had missed targets set by the UN's Second Development Decade by wide margins. Its GDP annual growth rate was 4.5 percent instead of the target of 6.0; its export was 2.8 percent instead of 7 percent; its agricultural growth rate was 1.6 percent instead of the target rate of 4 percent; while manufacturing grew at 6 percent instead of the target of 8 percent. The only macroeconomic aggregate whose performance bested the UN benchmark target was imports. The growth rate per annum in this sector was 10 percent, surpassing the 7 percent UN target.[31]

Against this backdrop were calls by the global south for a new world order, and the ECA was instrumental in coming up with three development blueprints for the continent. The first was the 1976 *Revised Framework of Principles for the Implementation of the New International Order in Africa*. Three years later, at the colloquium on "Perspectives of Development and Economic Growth in Africa up to the year 2000" convened in Monrovia in 1979 by the OAU, the ECA's 1976 blueprint became the "intellectual and theoretical foundation" of the OAU's Monrovia Declaration. A year later, at the OAU's second extraordinary summit in Nigeria, the OAU transformed the Monrovia Declaration into the Lagos Plan of Action and the Final Act of Lagos in 1980 (LPA), by setting itself to achieving the goal of economic integration of Africa by the year 2000, through the creation of an African Economic Community (AEC).

So early in the crisis in the mid-1970s the ECA made attempts at crafting an autonomous development agenda for Africa. According to

Professor Adebayo Adedeji, the ECA head at the time, the Revised Framework (on which the Monrovia Declaration and the LPA were subsequently built) postulated four fundamental development principles: "self-reliance, self sustainment, the democratization of the development process, and a fair and just distribution of the fruit of development through the progressive eradication of unemployment and mass poverty."[32] Most importantly, these blueprints identified the vulnerability of African economies to the harsh external environment as immediate culprits of Africa's underdevelopment. However, any early optimism attached to the ECA's policy autonomy in crafting endogenous economic growth models for Africa was short lived. Barely a year after LPA, the World Bank published a report titled "Accelerated Development in Sub-Saharan Africa." Authored by Elliot Berg, the report (often called the Berg Report) turned the LPA argument on its head and argued that Africa was performing poorly because of state interference in market and price allocation. According to the Berg Report, Africa was missing "three major policy actions that are central to any growth-oriented program: more suitable trade and exchange-rate policies; increased efficiency of resource use in the public sector, and improvement in agricultural policies."[33] The World Bank argued further that it was necessary to adopt orthodox economic policies because they would "unleash markets so that competition can help improve the allocation of resources ... [by] getting price signals right and creating a climate that allows businesses to respond to those signals in ways that increase the returns to investment."[34]

Much has been written on the Berg Report and LPA debate, so the details will not be recounted here.[35] The point worth making is that the World Bank and the other IEOs made neoliberal orthodoxy their preferred policy and were openly hostile to the development paradigms that were inspired by ECA, specifically the LPA. It also did not help much that on the home front Africa's economies were managed largely by authoritarian rulers, whilst globally the apparent triumph of the market and neoliberal politics was evidenced by the growing crisis in the political economy of the Eastern Bloc countries. These factors put the BWI's twin concepts of "rolling back the state" and "unleashing the markets" at a distinct advantage. Professor Adedeji, the ECA executive secretary whose tenure produced most of the above-mentioned blueprints, later lamented:

> In many cases, our friends and development partners have been either unwilling or reluctant to grant us the elementary right to perceive for ourselves what is good for us and to assist us in

realizing our perceived goals and objectives. Often, they appear more interested in foisting on us their own perceptions and goals. When it comes to Africa, the outsiders have always behaved as if they know better than Africans what is good for Africa, and the result is that without the needed co-operation and support, Africa has particularly always been derailed from pursuing relentlessly and vigorously the agenda it has set for itself, whether it is the Monrovia Strategy, the Lagos Plan of Action or the Final Act of Lagos.[36]

No matter the limitations of the LPA framework, and there were plenty of critics, it marked a serious attempt by the ECA to advance a normative policy agenda for Africa's development, unencumbered by the dictates of the BWIs.

Throughout the years since the IEOs got African states to adopt the neoliberal reformist policies, the ECA has been involved in half-hearted attempts to formulate "alternative" development platforms for Africa. Among these are: Africa's Priority Program for Economic Recovery 1986–90 (APPER) which was later converted into the UN Program of Action for Africa's Economic Recovery and Development (UN–PAAERD) (1986); the African Alternative Framework to Structural Adjustment Program for Socio-Economic Recovery and Transformation (AAF-SAP) (1989); the African Charter for Popular Participation for Development (1990); and the United Nations New Agenda for the Development of Africa in the 1990s (UN-NADAF) (1991). The ECA also had its fingerprints on the preparation of the NEPAD document and has an office to coordinate with NEPAD (to be discussed later).

The problem with these latter initiatives is that they have provided no real intellectual leadership or challenge to the neoliberal agenda (pushed by the BWIs) as the universally applicable paradigm of development. Indeed, it can be argued that the ECA's development documents, since the mid-1980s, while being critical of the BWIs' orthodox economic reform policies in Africa, are at the end of the day still firmly embedded in neoliberal policies. For example, the ECA's AAF-SAP (1989), is usually singled out by some as an "alternative framework" to the BWIs model. Green saw AAF-SAP as "a step toward molding official and academic African analysis toward an African based strategic framework and, perhaps, toward setting the foundations for more serious strategic and conceptual dialogue between the [World] Bank and SSA countries."[37] But others view AAF-SAP as unoriginal and full of contradictions. As Jeffery Herbst noted, "despite its title, [the ECA failed to] provide a new framework of analysis for its proposals.

Instead, what the AAF-SAP does is adopt the World Bank's framework of neoclassical microeconomics and then simply argue that there are exceptions to the model. This partial departure from the orthodoxy produces considerable confusion in the ECA's analysis, most notably in its view of the market."[38] Be that as it may, the AAF-SAP died on arrival because its legitimacy, as an alternative to BWI orthodoxy, did not convince many. Even the ECA's constituencies, the African states, by as early as 1986, while still critical of the structural constraints in the global economy were admitting publicly the soundness of the orthodox economic reforms of the BWIs. The OAU's Africa's Submission to the Special Session of the United Nations General Assembly on Africa's Economic and Social Crisis, for example, explicitly endorsed many of the World Bank reforms.[39]

The African leaders' decision to succumb to the demands of the BWIs, and remain noncommittal to ECA's economic growth paradigms, might have been due to the economic strictures of debt or lack of foresight and confidence in alternative models. For Ambassador Arkhurst, the Ghanaian delegate at the UN who was involved in the establishment of the ECA, the organization has been a disappointment. To him "The ECA has not lived up to its mandate because the African states have failed to use it. The African members of the ECA are supposed to establish the agenda of the ECA, to address African economic problems. To be able to do this the African states must establish an economic agenda for their countries and for the continent. I am not aware that this has been done to any great extent."[40]

The ADB and Africa's development discourse

English and Mule made a rather astute observation on the role between development banks in development when they wrote that:

> The ultimate goal of a commercial bank is profitability, and this is basically determined by the quantity and quality of loans it finances. The situation is more complicated for a development bank, as profitability is not the only measure of success. While it is expected to remain profitable (or at least cover costs, including potential losses from doubtful loans), its raison d'être is to promote development. At best, development impact must be assessed at several levels, at worst, it opens up the debate to conflicting opinions on what development really means. In addition, the development bank will often be confronted with a trade-off between development and financial soundness. This opens the potential debate still

further, begging the question as to the appropriate weight to be assigned to these twin objectives.[41]

At the heart of this statement is that development banks are responsible for both the theory and praxis of development. While English and Mule place less emphasis on the contentious issue of which development models work best, this is extremely crucial in the African context, where most development indicators have shown worsening conditions.

In the long term, the ADB, like other development banks, is positioned as a think tank. It has to create and accumulate the resources that would make it a center for information and knowledge. It should be an institution that creates strategy as well as puts its plans into action for the socioeconomic development of Africa. The call here is that besides serving as a regional development bank, ADB has the responsibility to serve as the leading voice for Africa on African and global issues. In short, to be a leading center of analysis and advice in the area of development policy. It is this role of ADB, as a knowledge intermediary, more than that of its financial intermediation functions, which constitutes the bulk of this section. The ADB is clearly not oblivious to the fact that it needs to be more proactive in the provision of economic knowledge and policy. The Bank acknowledges that the experience of most African countries

shows that development finance may be a necessary but not a sufficient condition for development. After nearly four decades of channeling development finance into African countries, they are poorer in per capita income terms today than they were at independence. After showing great growth potential in the immediate post-independence period, much of Africa suffered from negative per capita GDP growth for most of the four decades that followed.[42]

Unfortunately, the surrender to the dominant/core neoliberal thinking that has been characteristic of the ECA since the mid-1980s applies to the ADB as well. This is not surprising because strictly speaking IEOs are not economically neutral; they are political entities. Political dynamics between the organization's stakeholders, as well as the domestic sensitivities and demands of borrowing member states are all too often the norm in IEOs. African IEOs are no exception. The ADB in particular, is hampered by organizational hobbles, such as lack of professionalism, technical expertise and rivalries between the African and non-African executive shareholders. But as far as development dialogue goes the ADB, the "leading development institution in Africa" has done anything but lead. To be sure, the Bank conducts and disseminates its research findings through publications and conferences. It also provides policy advice to African governments (see Chapter 2).

The trouble is that the Bank has not been able to come up with an alternative analytical framework to the orthodox economic reform policies. The ADB can be said to have a development theory deficit. Having no economic development model that it could call its own, it has always had to play second fiddle to the policy advice of other IEOs, particularly the IMF and World Bank.[43] In the face of evidence that shows that the results of these orthodox economic reform policies have not been stellar, one would hope that the ADB would conduct its own problem-oriented research and examine the causes and dimensions of economic growth, and of poverty, amongst many other development issues.

When one compares the resources for research at the ADB to that of the World Bank and IMF, the absence of a vibrant research environment becomes very glaring. In 2000, the research divisions of the World Bank and IMF boasted about 100 professional research (and support) staff, while the ADB had only four personnel dedicated to research.[44] Writing for the Bank in 2006, The Center for Global Development (CGD) observed that "intellectually, the Bank is not yet living up to its core mandate of providing leadership and an African voice on the crucial global issues affecting Africa today."[45] Unfortunately, rather than providing the sort of intellectual leadership required to address Africa's development challenges, the ADB waits to take its cue from the external IEOs. The intellectual vacuum created as a result of ADB's absence of leadership on development has practical implications. The impact is most obvious when it comes to the area of policy-based lending. The ADB, having no alternative development framework, has had to collaborate with, and follow the lead of, the World Bank and IMF strategy on the application of conditionalities prior to loan disbursements. From 1989 to 1992 for example, only three of ADB's policy-based loans were not cofinanced with the World Bank or the IMF.[46] It is quite odd however, that as the premier financial and development institution of Africa, the ADB is hardly singled out when the contentious issue of donor conditionalities in Africa is raised. But this is hardly surprising to English and Mule. To them, ADB's implicit endorsement of the World Bank neoliberal orthodoxy "may have played a role in legitimizing the associated reforms in a way that no non-African organization could."[47] They go on to add that "it is not easy to work in Africa and no donor has a shining record, but the ADB Group has not done enough to reduce the risks and to shift the odds in its favor. There is very little evidence that its special African character is being put to good advantage to do things differently, and better, than other donors."[48]

NEPAD and Africa's development discourse

In spite of—or perhaps because of—the fact that it is the latest African IEO, NEPAD has generated very intense and often severe debate. Some criticisms have focused on the undemocratic nature by which the framework was created[49] and others have questioned the originality of NEPAD and the implications of its unabashed neoliberal orientation.[50] The latter critique is more germane to this discussion as a foreground to the conceptual framework and underlining economic philosophy on which NEPAD is crafted. NEPAD seeks an "increased Africa integration" with the global economy through a partnership primarily with the G-8 and the donor community at large. The vision of NEPAD requires African states to adhere to measured political and economic benchmarks in exchange for international aid. The "partnership" between African states and the donor community is envisioned more as a pact. Politically, African states pledge allegiance to democracy, accountability and good governance through a peer review process (see APRM in Chapter 2) and economically they would continue to pursue orthodox reform policies that are rooted in idea of minimal interference in markets and maximum promotion of private capital. In exchange, the donor community would help end Africa's marginalization in the global economy by forgiving debts, giving aid, providing better market access, and creating opportunities that would transform the power relations between Africa and the North.

By accepting the market-centered view of development as a given, NEPAD offers nothing new as far as the discourse of African development is concerned. As Adesina and his colleagues have rightly noted, "NEPAD rehashes the same policy instruments that have deepened Africa's structural crisis during the 25 years of IMF/World Bank structural adjustment. Its narrative conflates the ideological claims of the leading commissars of neo-liberalism."[51] NEPAD has been criticized by African intellectuals and the civil society at large. A network of African scholars meeting in Ghana on 23–26 April 2002 lambasted NEPAD as a flawed economic blueprint that "will reinforce the hostile external environment and the internal weaknesses that constitute the major obstacles to Africa's development challenges."[52] Also, in July 2002, members of some 40 African social movements, trade unions, youth and women's organizations, and NGOs, amongst others, rejected

NEPAD and called for a more legitimate African program that involves citizen participation. (see the African Civil Society Declaration on NEPAD, Appendix 1).

African IEOs: The end of history?

Given the lock in economic thinking by African IEOs, it is tempting not to reference Francis Fukuyama's essay "The End of History?," in which he argued that the advent of Western liberal democracy may signal the "the end point of mankind's ideological evolution."[53] Does the African IEOs' embrace of neoliberalism represent the final form of economic thinking in Africa? As if to affirm the mantra that "there is no alternative" to the economic logic of neoliberalism, all three African IEOs have committed themselves to increased coordination and cooperation, mainly around NEPAD. The ECA and ADB, in recent years, have renewed their desire to work more closely and strengthen their mutual collaboration. In April 2003, for instance, ECA and ADB started synchronizing their annual legislative meetings in a bid to adopt common platforms and strategies on development. The ECA, in August 2006 created a special division and unit dedicated solely to the support of NEPAD: the NEPAD and Integration Division (NRID) and the NEPAD support unit, located in the NRID. The ECA and the NEPAD secretariat currently have a memorandum of understanding (MOU) in place to advance joint efforts in support of the implementation of NEPAD. Some areas of focus outlined in the MOU include joint and strategic research, resource mobilization, capacity development, communication outreach and advocacy. The ADB too has established a liaison office with the NEPAD secretariat. The ADB's NEPAD unit is under the direct supervision of the Bank's vice-president, and assists in the provision of technical assistance and advisory services to NEPAD. The AU is contemplating incorporation of NEPAD into its structures.

Of course, the architects and supporters of NEPAD view it (market emphasis notwithstanding) as a more "mature" framework than past African-initiated development blueprints. They point out that NEPAD's embrace of the UN Millennium Development Goals, its assessment of the capacities of states and markets in Africa, and the shared accountability between Africa and the industrialized countries make it a more pragmatic paradigm. For others, especially those who view the LPA as an authentic African alternative to neoliberalism, any talk of NEPAD as more rooted in realism than other African initiatives is a rewrite of history. As ECA's Adedeji Adebayo, one of the brains behind LPA, observes, "the protagonists of NEPAD should never forget that it was this (neoliberal) model that exacerbated the dependency syndrome of the African economies and at the same time led to mass pauperization and deprivation of the African people." Coordination and cooperation among African IEOs is a good thing but it ought to make a meaningful contribution to the development discourse of Africa. The beginnings of which would occur once African IEOs became more open to pluralism in their economic thinking, rather than accepting outright the neoliberal paradigm as the only the model of growth. Indeed, it is imperative that African IEOs reclaim the intellectual high ground when it comes to the continent's economic destiny by offering alternatives not based solely on the market and prices but ones that also involve the active participation of the state and seriously envision a continental economic community.

2 Structure and activities of the African IEOs

To understand the role of African IEOs it is useful to examine the day-to-day workings of the organizations discussed in this volume. While there is clearly overlap in the missions of these groups, there is also substantial difference in both the structures and missions of the African IEOs. This is due to both the variation in goals of these organizations, but it is also largely a product of the historical context in which each organization arose. This chapter will examine each of these organizations in turn to provide a comparison of the work that each does, and to provide some of the historical background that have shaped these institutions.

ECA

Established in 1958, ECA's member states are the 53 African nations, represented by their ministers of finance and economic planning. The ECA structure is comprised of a commission, government ministers from member states as well as other policy-making groups, a secretariat, and sub-regional development centers. The economic and finance ministers from member states meet every two years at a conference to deliberate issues for the ECA. The conference of ministers carries out the responsibility of the Commission to promote unified action for Africa's economic and social development. In particular, the conference debates general policy and prioritizes the Commission's programs, addresses inter-African and international economic policy, and recommends certain actions to member states accordingly. There are two primary conferences: a conference of ministers of finance, and a conference of ministers of economic and social development and planning. They meet in alternate years. Providing guidance and assistance to the conferences are five intergovernmental committees of experts, one each from the sub-regional development centers of Central Africa, East

Africa, North Africa, Southern Africa, and West Africa. These groups of experts meet annually as a Technical Preparatory Committee of the Whole, founded in 1979 to report to the Commission on issues addressed by the Conference. There are also seven other committees that deal with more specific matters, namely, women and development; development information; sustainable development; human development and civil society; industry and private sector development; natural resources and science and technology; and regional cooperation and integration.

The main administrative body of the ECA is the secretariat. It organizes the meeting of the conference of ministers and of the Commission's subsidiary bodies. It also executes resolutions and implements programs adopted by the Commission. Paragraphs 17–19 of ECA's terms of reference stipulate that the secretariat be headed by an executive secretary, who is appointed by the secretary-general of the United Nations. (The ECA executive secretaries have hailed mainly from West Africa—see Table 2.1.) The executive secretary, as well as his deputy and staff are therefore considered members of staff of the UN and the headquarters of the Commission and its secretariat is to be located in Africa. The secretariat, which has undergone numerous restructuring, initially had nine major divisions with sub-units:[1] the Trade, Fiscal and Monetary Affairs Division, the Centre for Economic Co-operation, the National Resources and Transport Division, the Industry and Housing Division, the Research and Statistics Division, the Population Program Center, the Human Resources Development Division, the ECA/FAO Joint Agricultural Division, and the Administration, Conferences and General Services Division.

Presently, the secretariat has been reorganized to become a lean organization. Besides the office of the executive secretary, there are five

Table 2.1 ECA executive secretaries (1959–present)

Name	Country	Tenure
Mr. Abdoulie Janneh	Gambia	2005–present
Mr. Kingsley Amoako	Ghana	1995–2005
Mr. Layashi Yaker	Algeria	1992–1995
Mr. Issa Diallo	Guinea	1991–1992
Mr. Adebayo Adedeji	Nigeria	1975–1991
Mr. Robert K. A. Gardiner	Ghana	1961–1975
Mr. Mekki Abbas	Sudan	1959–1961

Source: ECA website, www.uneca.org, and other annual reports.

main divisions: Information, Science and Technology for Development; Governance and Public Administration; Gender and Social Development; Food Security and Sustainable Development; and Trade, Economic Development and Regional Integration.

ECA has projected that its total funding requirement for the three-year period 2007–2009 will amount to $278.3 million. Of this amount, $177.8 million is to be funded through the regular budget of the Commission, and the remaining $100.5 million will come from extra budgetary resources provided by ECA donors.[2] ECA has offices located in the five sub-regions in Africa: Central Africa (Yaoundé, Cameroon); East Africa (Kigali, Rwanda); North Africa (Tangier, Morocco); Southern Africa (Lusaka, Zambia); and West Africa (Niamey, Niger).

Activities

The ECA has been involved in a number of activities since its inception. Much of the discussion that follows on ECA's activities describes the pattern of recent policy initiatives and thus may not align neatly with the major structural divisions that have been in existence since 2006, when the organization undertook reforms. As part of a $25 billion UN System-wide Special Initiative on Africa, the ICT, Science and Technology Division (ISTD) of the ECA has been charged with harnessing information for development by strengthening the capacity and use of knowledge systems, such as spatial databases. It is also charged with implementing the African Information Society Initiative (AISI), which is designed to build an information and communications infrastructure. The AISI has its roots in a 1996 resolution (812-XXXI) adopted by the ECA Conference of Ministers requesting the Commission to "constitute a high level work group to develop an action plan on ICTs to accelerate socio-economic development in Africa."

ISTD is also responsible for enhancing and disseminating statistical databases, focusing on library and documentation services to increase access to information, and improving geo-information systems for the purpose of sustainable development. More generally, the ECA promotes the liberalization of the telecommunications sector in member states and the importation of computers to enhance information services in Africa. The ECA serves as the manager of the Ethiopia-based Information Technology Center for Africa (ITCA), and it administers the Partnership for Information and Communication Technologies in Africa. ECA also works to improve statistical databases throughout Africa by offering aid to member states for census-taking and demographic data analysis. It offers training for demographers at the Regional

Institute for Population Studies in Ghana and at the Institut de Formation et de Recherche Demographique in Cameroon. The ECA is also involved in informing population policies and development planning by organizing and disseminating information on demographics and development. The ECA encourages member states to use information systems as a governmental tool by, for example, establishing the African Virtual Library and Information Network in 1999 and launching the annual Africa Knowledge Networks Forum in 2000. Much of the work of the ICTD was formerly handled by the Development Information Services Division (DISD).

In August 2006, the ECA established the Governance and Public Administration Division (GPAD) to "improve governance and development management to enhance national capacity and capability" of its member states. GPAD also provides support for the Africa Peer Review Mechanism (APRM) process, an AU system designed to encourage good governance (see Box 2.1 for more information on the APRM). The ECA also publishes the *African Governance Report* (*AGR*), a biannual publication that aims to assess and monitor progress toward good governance in African countries. The ECA also works to help governments, universities, and the public and private sector improve financial management through workshops, seminars and conferences. This entails assistance in improving policymaking and analysis, addressing human resources and skill shortages, and promoting social development among the youth, disabled and elderly. Specific actions toward these goals include the first African Development Forum in 1999 to create a framework for effective and sustainable development throughout the continent, involving both the public and private sectors. The ECA also hosted the African Governance Forum in 1998 as part of the UN System-wide Special Initiative on Africa to promote development in Africa. Additionally, ECA supports the development of an efficient public sector and a civil society with greater popular participation. It does this by disseminating best practices, reviewing and reforming civil services, and promoting stronger local governments and less centralization. The ECA aims to enhance the dialogue between governments and their citizens, with a strong emphasis on improved information technology, databases, and communications.

Another unit of the ECA, the Gender, Economic, and Social Policy Division, focuses on assisting member states with general economic analysis, fiscal management, trade liberalization, and regional integration and planning. The unit also covers trade and debt, social policy and poverty issues. The ECA offers assistance to its members through

Box 2.1 The African Peer Review Mechanism (APRM)

To ensure that the policies and practices of African countries are in conformity with the agreed values of NEPAD, the creators of NEPAD have established a voluntary self-monitoring mechanism, the African Peer Review Mechanism (APRM). The process entails periodic reviews by a Country Review Team (APR team) that visits participating countries in four policy areas, namely Democracy and Political Governance, Economic Governance and Management, Corporate Governance, and Socio-Economic Development. Confidential reports by the APR team are then handed to the subject governments, and a program of action for improvements in the policy areas is agreed on and made public.

Collectively, the heads of state or government of the countries that have acceded to the APRM are referred to as the APR Forum, and act as the highest decision making authority in the APRM. A Panel of Eminent Persons (APR Panel) oversees the review process to ensure integrity, consider reports and make recommendations to the APR Forum. There is also an APRM secretariat (APR Secretariat) that provides secretarial, technical, coordinating and administrative support for the APRM. The APR Secretariat will eventually have researchers and consultants in each of the four policy areas of the APRM, outlined above.

So far 23 countries have signed up for APRM. Reviews of five countries—Ghana, Rwanda, Kenya, South Africa, and Algeria—have been completed. APRM country reviews are in their planning stages for Egypt, Mauritius, Uganda, and Nigeria.

Source: NEPAD website: www.nepad.org

special programs that foster growth in the job market and investments in education and health. As part of its analysis, the Commission publishes annual reports: the *Survey of Economic and Social Conditions in Africa* and the *Economic Report on Africa*. Regarding gender policy, the ECA looks to aid women in the economy by improving their access to resources, opportunities and decision making.[3] The African Center for Gender and Development (ACGD) was founded in 1975 by the ECA specifically for these purposes. The ACGD in October 2004 launched the African Gender and Development Index (AGDI) to provide African policymakers and their partners with tools to monitor progress toward gender equality and women's advancement. The ECA also hosts the African Center for Women, which seeks to include women in the Commission's programs, and monitors regional efforts for the advancement of women in African society and economy.

The ECA also works to promote sustainable development through institutions and policies pertaining to food production, food security, population, the environment, and human settlement. It supports scientific and technological efforts toward this end. The ECA monitors these issues with such periodical publications as the *Human Development in Africa Report* and the *Sustainable Development Report on Africa*, which was launched in the 2004–5 biennium. The ECA works to educate member states by shedding light on the relationships between population, food security, the environment, and sustainable development. The ECA also advises the UN on development-related strategies, putting forth African perspectives in the formulation of policy.

The ECA conducts studies on domestic trade, intra-African trade, transnational corporations, gender mainstreaming, enhancing state-trading organizations, debt relief, and development financing. The ECA works on trade issues and regional integration via its sub-regional developments centers of Central, East, North, Southern, and West Africa. It issues an *Annual Report on Regional Integration*. As mentioned in the previous chapter, the ECA in 2006 established the NEPAD and Regional Integration Division to consolidate its regional integration efforts and to provide institutional support for NEPAD. ECA currently provides support for NEPAD initiatives such as the Comprehensive African Agricultural Development Program (CAADP), ICT, trade negotiation, infrastructure, water, and the APRM. This division also concerns itself with intra-African transportation, mining industry issues, energy, and water resources. With the aid of the World Bank, the ECA coordinates the Sub-Saharan Africa Transport Program, which includes the regional Road Management Initiative to promote cooperation between the public and private sectors for more efficient road infrastructure management and maintenance. Better urban transport services and more cost-effective services for shippers are also goals of this program. As for mining issues, the ECA offers support to the Southern African Mineral Resources Development Center and the Central African Mineral Development Center.

The ECA also deals with energy issues through its Energy Program, which helps members to develop their energy resources and create policies design to stave off energy crises. The ECA is also the secretariat of the UN's Energy/Africa Initiative, which aims to facilitate information and knowledge sharing among the UN, private companies, NGOs, the energy sector and research institutions. The ECA promotes the cultivation of water sharing by assessing resources and usage and developing rivers and lakes to be used by more than one state. Again, the goal of the ECA is to promote regional integration as well as integration in the global economy, and it does so by working with member states on cooperative agreements as well as with the WTO, IMF, World Bank and the EU. The ECA also advocates South–South cooperation, to promote ties with other developing regions, such as Asia and Latin America. Issues involving trade and regional integration are now coordinated under the new Trade, Finance and Economic Development Division (TFED), which was established in 2006 to better coordinate macroeconomic, trade, and financial policy. This new division comprises the Industry and Sectoral Policies Section, the Financing Development Section, the Trade and International Negotiations Section, the Macroeconomic Analysis Section, and the African Trade Policy Center (ATPC).

In March 2006, the executive secretary of the ECA established a task force to provide him with recommendations to help shape new directions for the Commission. This was not the first time that the ECA had undertaken reform efforts (recent restructuring efforts occurred in 1991, 1996, and 2002), however; the ECA argued that repositioning was necessary due to ongoing reforms in the UN system at the time as well as the renewed global commitment to improving Africa's development prospects. The task force completed its work in June 2006, having consulted with ECA staff, its member states and partners such as the AU, ADB, UNDP and its sister agencies, the RECs, and ECA's bilateral partners. Among the key recommendations of the task force was a need for more emphasis to be placed on knowledge generation and networking, advocacy and advisory services, and technical cooperation. The task force stressed that within the two pillars of ECA's work—promoting regional integration in support of the AU vision and priorities and helping to meet Africa's special needs and the emerging global challenges—the Commission will focus on the following thematic areas: regional integration, infrastructure and trade; meeting the MDGs with a special emphasis on poverty reduction and growth, sustainable development and gender; promoting good governance and popular participation; ICT, and science and technology (S&T) for development; and statistical development.

Recent ECA initiatives underscore the new impetus and direction of the organization. The ECA, in December 2007, announced the establishment of an African center for climate policy studies. The ECA believes that ongoing and projected climate change will negatively affect the efforts of African countries to achieve the targets of the MDGs and eradicate poverty. The proposed center would then serve an indispensable role by providing African countries with analytical work and the capacity for mainstreaming climate-related concerns in the frameworks of their development policies, strategies and plans. In a similar vein, the ECA, in March 2008, convened the first ever "Science with Africa" to raise the level and range of participation and collaboration of African science-based entities in international research and development (R&D) projects, and also to inform new science diplomacy within Africa. Finally, a new forum, the Coalition for Dialogue on Africa (CoDA) is also in the works; it will be a merger of the "Big Table" (Africa–OECD ministerial consultation) and the Global Coalition for Africa, which has been wound up.

Based on the recommendation of the task force (whose work was incorporated into the ECA 2007–2009 Business Pan and fully endorsed by the AU), it appears that the ECA, moving forward, will place its emphasis on supporting efforts that lead to: poverty alleviation, reversing the marginalization of Africa in the globalization process, and the empowerment of women.

ADB

The ADB was established in 1964, and began operations in July 1966, with the aim of financing economic and social development in African countries. Article 2(1) of the charter of the Bank states that its functions are, inter alia:

- to use the resources at its disposal for the financing of investment projects and programs relating to the economic and social development of its members (giving special priority to projects or programs which by their nature or scope concern several members and projects or programs designed to make the economies of its members increasingly complementary and to bring about an orderly expansion of their foreign trade);
- to undertake, or participate in, the selection, study and preparation of projects, enterprises and activities contributing to such development;
- to mobilize and increase in Africa, and outside Africa, resources for the financing of such investment projects and programs.

The ADB has 77 member countries; all 53 states in Africa are members, as well as 24 non-regional members, who do not borrow from the

Bank (see Appendix 2 for a list of the eligible countries for each fund). The non-regional members are: Argentina; Austria; Belgium; Brazil; Canada; China; Denmark; Finland; France; Germany; India; Italy; Japan; Korea; Kuwait; Netherlands; Norway; Portugal; Saudi Arabia; Spain; Sweden; Switzerland; the United Kingdom; and the United States of America. The ADB has five associate institutions, which it helped establish: African Reinsurance Corporation (Africa-Re), African Export-Import Bank (Afreximbank), Association of African Development Finance Institutions (AADFI), Shelter-Afrique (Société pour l'habitat et le logement territorial en Afrique), and Société Internationale Financière pour les Investissements et le Développement en Afrique (SIFIDA).

The entire organization is called the ADB Group (or the Bank in this volume), and it has three components: the African Development Bank (ADB), the African Development Fund (ADF), and the Nigeria Trust Fund (NTF). The African Development Bank was set up in 1967; this component of the ADB group, also known as the hard-window of the Bank, offers loans at variable interest rates, plus a commission charge of 0.75 percent. The rates are adjusted twice a year. Loan approvals amounted to US$1.24 billion for 34 loans in 2005, compared with $2.35 billion for 23 loans in the previous year. The African Development Fund (ADF) was established in 1972 and began operations in 1974. Known as the soft loan arm of the ADB Group, ADF offers interest-free loans geared toward low-income African states. Repayment is stretched out over 50 years, and there is a 10-year grace period within that time span. The ADF charges 0.75 percent annually. This window is financed largely by grants from non-regional members. In 2005, ADF made out 65 loans and grants to the tune of US$2.03 billion. The Nigeria Trust Fund (NTF) was founded in 1976 by the Bank and the Nigerian government; which is the largest share-holder of the ADB. NTF loans are geared toward financing projects in partnership with other lenders. The NTF promotes African trade by disseminating information about financial institutions in Africa and international ones that support African trade. Loans offered by the NTF are for a 25-year period, and carry a 0.75 percent commission fee, and 4 percent interest fees. Three loans were approved during 2005 amounting to US$4.6 million. The entire ADB group, since it began operations up till 2005, has approved approximately US$55.2 billion in loans and grants. Of that amount agriculture received the largest proportion of assistance (18.1 percent), transport received 16.5 percent, multi-sector activities 15.2 percent, and finance 13.3 percent. In 2005, the Bank approved US$3.2 billion in loans and grants, with Egypt and

Tunisia being the largest beneficiaries. (For a summary of the Bank's loan activities, see Appendix 2.)

The administration of the ADB group is made up of a board of governors, a board of directors, and officers. The board of governors is the supreme policymaking organ of the ADB Group. The board of governors creates policy, admits new members and approves increases in capital. There is one governor nominated to the board per member state. An alternate governor (or the governor of a state's central bank) is also nominated. The governors on the board are typically finance or economic ministers in their home state, and exercise their voting powers to reflect the interests of their home countries. Each member country in the ADB has an equal number of basic votes in addition to a number of votes proportional to its paid-in shares. The decisions of the board are generally made through deliberations and consensus rather than through the exercise of voting powers. The board of governors meets yearly to review past policy decisions and to deliberate on new policy issues initiated by board, the board of directors, or by the management of the Bank. The board of governors has the sole discretion in matters relating to the admission of new members, increase in the capital stock, amendments to the Articles of Agreement and the election of the board of directors and the president.

Each component of the Bank has its own directors. The board of directors for the African Development Bank (ADB) is composed of 18 members who are neither governors nor alternate governors. Six of the members are elected by the governors of non-regional member countries. Each director serves for three years, with a maximum of two terms. Members of the board of directors are responsible for the conduct of the general operations of the Bank, which include approving all loans, guarantees and equity investments, setting operational and financial guidelines, and approving annual borrowing programs. To facilitate its work the board has established five permanent committees: They are: the Committee on Administrative and Human Resources Policy Issues; the Audit and Finance Committee; the Committee on Operations and Development Effectiveness; the Committee on Administrative Matters concerning the Boards of Directors; and Committee of the Whole on the Budget. The board of directors of the ADF is composed of twelve directors (six directors and six alternate directors) drawn from ADB. The ADF board of directors is encouraged to invite other directors of the Bank to participate (as observers) in the discussion of any proposed project designed to benefit the country of which directors of the Bank are represented. ADF directors serve for three years and the term is renewable once, but terminates whenever a general increase in subscriptions becomes effective. The African Development Bank manages the Nigeria Trust Fund, on a delegated basis, through its own organization, services, and resources as may be necessary. The NTF's governor for the Bank is regularly consulted in the management of the Fund. Each loan or other form of financing granted out of the resources of the Fund must be approved by the board of directors of the Bank in accordance with the voting rules set forth in the Agreement establishing the African Development Bank in respect of its ordinary capital operations.

The daily operations of the Bank are the responsibility of the president, who takes his/her lead from the board of directors. The president is chairman of the board of directors and serves for a five-year term, which is renewable once. The leadership of the Bank group was restructured in 2001, leading to a rise in the number of vice-presidents from three to five. These VPs are responsible respectively for: Planning, Policy and Research; Corporate Management; Central and West Regional Operations; North, East and South Regional Operations; and Finance. These VPs are recommended by the president and appointed by the board of directors.

As of 31 January 2005, the Bank had 1,015 employees (exclusive of elected officers). These comprise 5 vice-presidents, 90 directors and managers, 556 professionals and 364 general services staff. In July 2006, another organizational structure mandated the president to supervise the following senior management: Chief Economist, Vice-Presidents of Finance, Corporate Services, Country and Regional Programs and Policy, Sector Operations, and Infrastructure, Private Sector and Regional Integration, Auditor General, General Counsel, Secretary-General, and an Ombudsman. Donald Kaberuka is the seventh elected president of ADB (see his biography in Box 2.2 and a list of ADB presidents in Table 2.2).

The ADB finances its operations in two ways. Regional and non-regional members provide the Bank with paid-in capital, generally payable in hard currencies (such as dollars or euros) or members pledge callable capital—essentially a promissory note—that amounts to much more than the paid-in capital. The Bank then uses the callable capital as collateral to borrow funds on the world capital markets to make loans to its members. The ADB has three main categories of funding: ordinary capital resources, concessional funds, and favorable conditions funds. Ordinary capital resources—handled by the ADB—come from borrowed funds from international capital markets and accumulated net income. Concessional funds—handled by the ADF—are geared toward low-income members who cannot borrow on the

Box 2.2 Current leaders of the major African economic institutions

1 Abdoulie Janneh—the ECA

On 20 September 2005, the UN secretary-general announced the appointment of Abdoulie Janneh as Executive Secretary of the Economic Commission for Africa.

Mr. Janneh had been serving since June 2000 as assistant secretary-general and UNDP's regional director for Africa. Prior to that, he held a number of senior positions in UNDP and its affiliated funds, including resident coordinator and resident representative in Ghana (1996–99) and Niger (1993–96), as well as deputy executive secretary of the United Nations Capital Development Fund (1990–93).

Under his leadership, the UNDP Bureau for Africa made significant contributions to the promotion of good governance, economic reform, the fight against HIV/AIDS, fair trade, crisis prevention and poverty eradication.

Mr. Janneh joined UNDP in 1979 as a development planner from the administration of his home country. He holds an M.A. in Urban and Regional Planning Studies from the University of Nottingham in England. He also graduated from Fourah Bay College, Sierra Leone (Engineering Science) and undertook postgraduate studies in Project Planning and Appraisal at the University of Bradford in England. Abdoulie Janneh is from Gambia and is fluent in English and French.

Source: ECA, www.uneca.org

2 Donald Kaberuka—The ADB

Donald Kaberuka is the seventh elected president of the African Development Bank Group, and took the oath of office on 1 September 2005.

He hails from Rwanda, but was educated in Tanzania and the United Kingdom where he obtained his M.Phil. (economics) and a Ph.D. in economics from Glasgow University in Scotland. Dr. Kaberuka worked for 12 years in the banking and financial services industry before he joined the government. Prior to his election he served as Rwanda's minister of finance and economic planning since 1997, and was responsible for that country's post-war reconstruction

(*Box continued on next page*)

and economic reform. In his capacity as minister of finance and economic planning, Dr. Kaberuka was governor for Rwanda at the World Bank, the International Monetary Fund (IMF) and the African Development Bank. He is fluent in English, French, and Swahili.

Source: ADB, afdb.org

3 Firmino Mucavele—NEPAD Secretariat

Firmino Mucavele was born in Mozambique on 16 January 1957, and has been the head of the NEPAD Secretariat since 1 August 2005. He holds a Ph.D. in food and resource economics from the University of Florida (USA) and also serves as a special adviser to the president of the Republic of Mozambique.

In 2000, Dr. Mucavele was part of a team of experts who provided direction for the third UN conference on Science and Technology for the development of Least Developed Countries. He was also instrumental in the drafting of the Millennium Africa Recovery Program (MAP), which was later transformed to NEPAD.

As an agricultural economist, Dr. Mucavele has consulted and/or worked for SADC, USAID, OXFAM, World Bank and Price Waterhouse Coopers, and numerous other international and national organizations.

Between the years 1994 and 2000, Dr. Mucavele was a professor and later dean at the Eduardo Mondlane University, Maputo, Mozambique. Dr. Mucavele is fluent in English, Portuguese, Spanish, and French.

Source: NEPAD secretariat, www.nepad.org

Table 2.2 The ADB presidents

Name	Country	Tenure
Mamoun Beheiry	Sudan	Nov. 1967–Aug. 1970
Abdelwahad Labidi	Tunisia	Aug. 1970–May 1976
Kwame Donkor Fordwor	Ghana	May 1976–July 1979
Goodall Gondwe	Malawi	July 1979–June 1980
Wila D. Mung' Omba	Zambia	June 1980–May 1985
Babacar N'diaye	Senegal	May 1985–Aug. 1995
Omar Kabbaj	Morocco	Aug. 1995–Sept. 2005
Donald Kaberuka	Rwanda	Sept. 2005–present

Source: *Annual Report* (various) www.afdb.org

market or the ADB's non-concessional terms. The 24 non-regional members are part of this development fund, which is replenished every three years. These concessional funds come from the ADB and member states—primarily non-regional—and periodic funding. The favorable conditions funds are managed by the NTF.

Activities

From its inception the Bank has set itself the goal of becoming the leading development institution in Africa. Not surprisingly, it has been involved in the financing of a plethora of development projects that range from agriculture, transportation, health, education, gender, and the environment, to name a few. The Bank does not finance military equipment; raw or manufactured tobacco; nuclear reactors, precious stones, or metals; or any environmentally hazardous product. In addition to granting loans and financing projects, the ADB, with the aim of generating direct foreign investment inflows and promoting small and medium-size enterprises, has renewed its efforts to promote capacity building initiatives and private sector development, and to the provide technical assistance, knowledge dissemination and policy advice to its regional members. In partnership with the IMF and the World Bank, the Bank was instrumental in establishing three major research and training institutes in Africa: the African Capacity Building Foundation (ACBF), the African Development Institute (ADI), and the Joint African Institute (JAI). The ACBF was established in 1991 to strengthen and develop institutional and human capacity in support of sustainable development activities. The ADI's goal is to enhance the administration of projects financed by the ADB. It also manages the ADB/Japan Fellowship program that provides scholarships to African students yearly, to undertake higher studies. The ADB/Japan Fellowship leads to the award of fellowships for master's degree studies at internationally recognized universities. The JAI was founded in 1999 for the purpose of providing training in economic policy and management and promoting capacity building.

Apart from sponsoring training and capacity building projects, the ABD has been involved in private sector development and promotion of business and investment culture. It realizes that there is much to do in this area because of the relatively weak and unstable economies in Africa. The Bank works by helping to build frameworks for private development, including micro-credit and savings services. Another way the ADB attempts to shore up the private sector is to try to stabilize public policies. The ADB assists its regional members in doing this by helping them to organize their business and financial laws and regulations, offering training and technical assistance, and providing access to international markets and foreign capital. For example, the ADB in 1986 helped to finance the Africa Project Development Facility. This facility aids business owners by providing advice and funding, and is managed by the Private Enterprise Partnership for Africa. Also, the Bank together with IFC and UNDP, in 1989, created the African Management Services Company (AMSCo), which provides management support and training to private companies in Africa. As of June 2008, the Bank had made over a $1 billion in annual private sector investments in Africa. Other business-related initiatives include the African Business Round Table (ABR), which comprises the CEOs of the largest corporations in Africa. The primary purpose of the ABR, which was created in 1990, is to promote trade and investment in Africa and bolster the private sector. The president of the ADB serves as the chairman of the ABR.

The ADB ensures policy coordination and effectiveness in its lending operations by engaging in a country policy dialogue via its *Country Strategy Paper* (CSP). CSPs are principal programming strategy documents prepared for each country every three years and updated annually to translate the performance-based resource allocation into an effective operational program. The Bank has also been involved in credit and debt negotiations on behalf of its regional members. One way it helps its members in this regard is to assist in the preparation of their poverty reduction strategy papers (PRSPs) for the BWIs. PRSPs describe a country's macroeconomic, structural and social policies over a three-year or longer horizon and are written up by a nation applying for a loan from the BWIs or when the nation is trying to get a lower interest rate on existing loans. The Bank also collaborates with the World Bank on debt relief for the heavily indebted poor countries (HIPCs). In September 2006, for example, the ADF established the Multilateral Debt Relief Initiative (MDRI). The MDRI, which was proposed by the G-8 at the Gleneagles summit on 8 July 2005, is expected to give beneficiary countries the opportunity to reduce their overall debt service payments and, through continued good performance, secure additional resource flows to help them attain the MDGs. It is estimated that 33 African member countries would benefit from the US$8.5 billion debt relief under the MDRI to be provided by the ADF. While the World Bank is a competitor of the ADB, the World Bank's executive and technical education programs are now open to the ADB's managers and staff. In addition, the ADB is partnering with the World Bank and others to pave the way for the adoption of sector investment programs by individual states. These programs enable coordination among partners by sector, which enhances regional effectiveness. The Bank is involved in a wide range of development research and dissemination activities. The Bank aims to be the central organ for economic knowledge and policy on Africa. To this end it publishes the *African Development Report*, the *African Development Review*, the *Economic Research Papers*, and various statistical publications. Perhaps in a bid to craft its own distinct economic development agenda, the ADB in November 2006 launched what will be an annual African Economic Conference series. Based on the Bank's 2003–7 strategic plan, which was approved by the board of directors in 2000, it appears the Bank will continue to allocate its resources to agriculture and sustainable rural development, with selective support given to the infrastructural development. The Bank will also continue to support economic integration schemes, such as NEPAD, and crosscutting issues such as the promotion of good governance, environmental protection, and gender concerns. The strategic plan emphasizes greater selectivity and targeting specific areas of intervention in the Bank's operations.

NEPAD

As noted in the previous chapter, NEPAD was formally launched in October 2001 during a meeting of African government heads in Nigeria. NEPAD has a four-tier governing structure: the AU heads of state, the Heads of State Implementation Committee (HSIC), the steering committee, and the NEPAD secretariat. The HSIC comprises 15 states (three states per AU region), reports to the AU every year, and is mandated to be the highest authority of the NEPAD implementation. The HSIC countries are: *Central Africa*: Cameroon, Gabon, and São Tomé and Príncipe; *East Africa*: Ethiopia, Mauritius, and Rwanda; *North Africa*: Algeria, Egypt, and Tunisia; *Southern Africa*: Botswana, Mozambique, and South Africa; *West Africa*: Mali, Nigeria, and Senegal. The steering committee of NEPAD is made up of personal representatives of the heads of state of the five NEPAD initiating states (Algeria, Egypt, Nigeria, Senegal, and South Africa). The steering committee develops terms of reference for identified programs and projects and directs the activities of the NEPAD secretariat.

The NEPAD organization (known as the secretariat) is a small full-time core staff based at the Development Bank of Southern Africa in Midrand, South Africa. The first chief executive officer of the secretariat was Wiseman Nkuhlu of South Africa (2001–5), and the second is Mozambican Firmino Mucavele (2005–present, see Box 2.2

for biography).[5] The secretariat is charged with the day-to-day functions of liaison, coordination, administration, and logistics in support of NEPAD. It is also mandated to outsource work on technical detail to prominent development agencies and/or continental experts. The staff is structured around five task teams, led by the representatives of the five founding member states, and charged with identifying and preparing actionable projects and programs. These are: the Peace, Security, Democracy and Political Governance Initiative (South Africa); the Economic and Corporate Governance/Banking and Financial Standards/Capital Flows Initiatives (Nigeria); the Market Access and Agriculture Initiatives (Egypt); the Human Resources Development Initiative (Algeria); and the Infrastructure Initiative (Senegal). As an African IEO therefore, the role of NEPAD (or specifically the secretariat) is to create policy ideas and assist with the coordination of programs approved by the AU, but it is not in itself an implementation agency. The UN allocated US $10.8 million to support NEPAD under its 2006–7 budget.

The main task of the NEPAD secretariat during the first few years (2001–5) of its formation was on advocacy and development of action plans for the six sectoral priorities viewed as essential parts of Africa's economic and social development. The sectoral priorities are economic governance, market access and agriculture, human development, infrastructure, science and technology, and environment and tourism. Key stakeholders such as African governments, the private sector community, and civil society, as well as the leaders of the G-8 countries, the United Nations and its agencies, amongst others, have been briefed on the main principles, objectives, and priorities of NEPAD. The initiatives carried out under the priority areas follows.

NEPAD has established three initiatives to deal with economic governance: the Capital Flows Initiative, Core Principles for Effective Banking Supervision, and Economic and Corporate/Political Governance Initiatives. The Capital Flows Initiative is intended to achieve the 7 percent annual growth rate that NEPAD has set as a goal, and to achieve the objective of cutting the number of Africans living in poverty by half by 2015. Capital flows must be increased in order to meet these targets, and so the Capital Flows Initiative focuses on increasing domestic savings, improving public revenue collection, lowering debt and overseas development assistance, private capitals flows, and better governance. The other economic governance initiatives of NEPAD set up guidelines and regulations that African states can adopt to foster economic growth and development. NEPAD has also instituted the APRM to encourage probity, transparency, and democratic accountability across the continent (see Box 2.1).

NEPAD has also created programs to achieve food security. Among these is the Comprehensive Africa Agriculture Development Program (CAADP). This program focuses on extending the area under sustainable land management and reliable water control systems, improving rural infrastructure and trade-related capacities for market access, and increasing food supply and reducing hunger. CAADP is aimed at assisting the launching of a green revolution in Africa. Additionally, NEPAD has set up frameworks for health, education, and information technology. Its health strategy targets preventable disease, disability, and death in order to work toward the goal of eradicating poverty. In education, NEPAD is devoted to creating strategies to reverse the brain drain, to bridge the education gap, and to develop higher education in Africa. It also created a market access action plan called the Millennium Partnership for the African Recovery Program. NEPAD also looks to bridge the information infrastructure gap by recommending investment in communication technologies. The "e-schools program," adopted by the HSGIC in 2003, is an initiative aimed at equipping all 600,000 primary and secondary schools in Africa with IT equipment and internet access within 10 years, in partnership with several large IT companies.

In an effort to increase overall African infrastructure stability, NEPAD has created strategies that would enhance all infrastructure sectors: roads, highways, airports, seaports, railways, waterways, and telecommunications facilities. NEPAD recognizes that this would require sustained foreign investment and capital, and has set up the Pan African Infrastructure Development Fund (PAIDF), with support from the Public Investment Corporation of South Africa, to finance high priority cross-border infrastructure projects. Two such projects being planned are the East African Submarine Cable System (EASSy), which seeks to connect the African continent with the rest of the world, and the African marine cable, which seeks to link the entire African continent with broadband technology. NEPAD has created a framework that addresses not only information infrastructures and computer access to aid socioeconomic development, but also biotechnology for sustainable development. The NEPAD Science and Technology Program emphasizes research in areas such as water science and energy. NEPAD also hopes to address climate change; conservation and sustainable use of coastal, marine, and freshwater resources; land degradation, drought and desertification; forests; environmental impact on health; biological diversity; environmental impact on poverty; managing wetlands; and eliminating stockpiled pesticides from Africa.

Unfortunately, NEPAD as an institution is in a limbo. AU heads do not want NEPAD to operate as a parallel organization and have tabled a motion to have NEPAD's structures merged within the AU system. The proposal to merge NEPAD with the African Union comes amid allegations of power struggles between presidents Abdoulaye Wade of Senegal, and South African Thabo Mbeki, both architects of NEPAD. The NEPAD secretariat, however, insists that NEPAD was designed to be an arm of the AU all along, and never as a parallel institution or implementation agency. Here is how Wiseman Nkuhlu, a former chief executive of NEPAD, described the role of NEPAD and the AU:

> in terms of the overall NEPAD strategy, implementation is the responsibility of national governments, Regional Economic Communities (RECs), and the AU organs. Therefore, the centre of activity should have shifted from the NEPAD secretariat to the implementers from 2004 onwards. Unfortunately this did not happen as planned because national governments and the RECs have been slow in building the institutional capacity they need in order to lead the implementation.[6]

Whether NEPAD eventually morphs into an AU entity, whether it remains as is, or whether it withers away remains to be seen. The AU heads of government agreed to take up this issue at their July 2008 meeting.

3 Toward a heterodox approach

A review of the activities of African IEOs suggests that rather than playing lead roles in the African development context, African IEOs have been unwilling or unable to extricate themselves from the ideological and policy dominance of the BWIs. It does not help that the majority of African governments, to whom the African IEOs report, have a natural proclivity to approve externally generated ideas of African IEOs. Why has the supply (from African IEOs) and demand (from African governments) for Africa's development strategies and policy orientations been so exogenously inclined? Why did the African IEOs follow the "Washington consensus" of neoliberalism instead of pursuing inward-looking strategies of collective self-reliance policies? More importantly, what can be done to overcome challenges to the enactment of heterodox policies?[1]

In trying to understand why African IEOs have not been more effective in opposing neoliberal policies (dictated and influenced by the BWIs) much of the discussion here takes place within the context of how capacity, autonomy, and accountability are operative in concrete situations. Do African IEOs have the capacity to carry out their own growth-oriented projects or are they hampered and/or hijacked by an accumulating class, financial constraints and ineffective bureaucracies? And finally, to what extent have African IEOs been agents of accountability to the overall societal needs that flow from their mandate, and how have they created opportunities for inclusiveness and participation of the broader publics, whom their policies affect directly?

ECA and policy development

As the premier institution responsible for the design, development and formulation of economic policies in Africa, the ECA cannot be found wanting in the discharge of its tasks. At issue is that the ECA, like the rest of the African IEOs, appears to have been co-opted over time by the World Bank and IMF, and has ended up producing policy recommendations that do not enhance the continent's political economy and development objectives. As noted in Chapter 1, the ECA has been instrumental in all the continent's overall landmark development blueprints since the 1980s. However, most of its proposals were rejected by the BWIs mainly on the grounds that the ECA's insistence on assigning a role for the state in the management of African economies was a recipe for further disaster. Lamenting the ECA's plight, its former head, Adebayo Adedeji, noted:

> all of these [ECA proposals] were opposed, undermined and jet-tisoned by the Bretton Woods Institutions and Africans were thus impeded from exercising the basic and fundamental right to make decisions about their future. This denial would have been amelio-rated if the African leaders had shown the commitment to carry out their own developmental agenda. But given excessive external dependence, their narrow political base, and their perennial failure to put their money where their mouth is, the implementation of these plans has suffered from benign neglect. Lacking the resources and the will to soldier on self-reliantly, they abandon their own strategies, including the two UN-PAARED and UN-NADAF, which were crafted jointly with the international community under the aegis of the United Nations.[2]

It has been noted that the ECA on its own does not have implementation capacity, so its ability to be an effective agent of development lies in the nature of policy influence that it has with its two constituents: the UN system and, especially, the African governments. As a UN body, its budget forms part of the overall United Nations budget and its secretariat is part of the staff of the UN's Department of Economic and Social Affairs. From the standpoint of developing policy, the ECA is required to submit for prior approval to UN ECOSOC, proposals which may have an important impact on the world as a whole. This is a vague requirement and one that should not prevent the ECA from advocating blueprints that would ultimately benefit Africans. As Akiwumi reminds us,

> the effect of this provision, which relates to proposals only which, even if they were to be in the more effective form of adopted resolu-tions, would still not be binding on the member states of the ECA, might well have led, on the part of the ECA, to a reluctance to

consider even the least of revolutionary steps designed to promote the economic development of Africa."[3]

Since the ECA lacks operational authority to carry out its own programs, its influence (and perforce the adoption of its development proposals) then rests mainly with African governments. But as presented in Chapter 1, the African stakeholders, while paying lip service to the LPA's inward-looking strategy of collective self-reliance, abandoned that African-owned development framework in favor of the externally derived model of neoliberalism packaged as structural adjustment policies. After repeatedly ditching the earlier ECA blueprints, African governments have now finally embraced the NEPAD, a neoliberal policy document which the ECA helped craft. This raises a couple of interesting possibilities on the contextual relationship between the ECA and African states. It can be argued that African states either did not have the confidence or political will to implement the ECA's earlier strategies. In other words, the African governments were disinterested in the ECA proposals because they were risky from a policy perspective. The corollary to this is that the ECA would have an open window of policy influence with African governments only when the analytical development framework proposed was mutually agreeable to both parties. Another scenario is that African states liked the policy ideas of the ECA but were constrained by financial and leadership resources to implement them. Given this context, the question of interest is: why did African governments commit to NEPAD and not the LPA?

Before turning to this question it must be noted that although the ECA lacks decisional autonomy it is not constrained in its ability to study, analyze, recommend, and propose development agendas for African governments. On this score, the ECA had, at least in the pre-Washington consensus era, fashioned policy frameworks that were based on a "holistic human development paradigm, not a narrow economic growth strategy."[4] It is worth repeating that the documents that the ECA produced, up until the LPA, stressed human investment as a key part of transforming African economies. The focus on human development in the LPA sets it apart from the neoliberal framework of the SAPs. After all, like most UN regional commissions, the ECA was created to provide a unique historical analysis of the continent's economic problems. As Yves Berthelot noted, this makes UN regional commissions more likely to "go against the neoclassical approach that, in its tendency to prescribe 'one-size-fits-all' policies, plays down the role of cumulative socioeconomic processes as a constraint on policymakers' freedom of action."[5] Needless to say, whatever policy space the ECA may have once had quickly evaporated once the dictates of the market and prices (pushed by the BWIs) became the dominant model of economic management in the early 1980s.

ADB and policy development

The question of capacity is germane to the work of the ADB because it, unlike the other African IEOs, has operational authority to implement its decisions. While most assessments show significant improvements in its staff capacity, the ADB still has operational issues that make it a secondary, rather than a primary, actor when it comes to policy influence. In terms of financial resources, the ADB remains a peripheral player in a crowded aid field. The Bank is only the sixth-largest source of official finance on the continent, providing just 6 percent of total resources.[6] Not having the requisite resources, the ADB has had to play junior partner to the BWIs. As English and Mule observed:

> The World Bank has a cast a long shadow over the ADB group. In every field or country the ADB Group has entered, the World Bank has already been operating and typically continues to operate with more staff, more funding, and more influence. The ADB Group has tried to establish its own identity, primarily by maintaining its African character and by increasing its annual loan commitments to the point where it would be a major player. Yet in almost every other respect, it has tended to replicate the World Bank, admittedly with considerable encouragement from the non-regional shareholders.[7]

Because of its weak capacity, the ABD's prestige and policy influence on African governments is quite negligible when compared to that accorded to the BWIs. African governments do not give the ADB high priority because of their own (the government's) scarce human capital. English and Mule write that "what human resources are available are more likely to be directed at the World Bank and the IMF, where the big money and bigger decisions reside. The ADB Group has been seen as a sympathetic and successful ally that can be relied upon and hence neglected."[8] The ADB has a long way to go before its resources and expertise are valued by both African governments and the donor community.

Due to this weak operational capacity, the ADB has not been intellectually independent of the BWIs. As noted in Chapter 2, the ADB has yet to deliver on its mandate as the leading African voice on the crucial global issues affecting Africa's development. According to Karen Mingst, the fact that the ADB "has not published a coherent theory of economic development" has diminished, and not enhanced, the Bank's credibility in the donor community.[9] English and Mule concur. To them, "Africans have the same right to sit at the donor table when adjustment is being discussed. However, the bilateral donors may have difficulty justifying their support to the ADB Group if they cannot point to a unique, contribution distinct from their own."[10] The unflattering results of the BWIs' development model in Africa make the need for an African perspective on development (from African IEOs) even more crucial.

With regards to accountability, the ADB answers to both its regional and non-regional members, though most evaluations have concluded that the expectations of its shareholders far exceed the Bank's capacity to deliver. One such independent evaluation warns that "shareholder pressures have muddied the Bank's mission, fragmented its operations, undermined its ability to make strategic choices, and, ultimately, made it a much less effective development agency than it could be."[11]

NEPAD and policy development

NEPAD, like the ECA, is not an implementation agency, and its capacity rests mainly with African governments. It almost seems redundant to restate that NEPAD is celebrated by the AU as an African-owned development blueprint in content and direction. This is not to suggest that there is unanimous consensus amongst AU leaders on NEPAD's promise. During the inauguration of NEPAD, AU leaders like Uganda's President Yoweri Museveni stressed that "beggars are tolerated, but they are not partners." Gambia's President Yahya Jammeh forecasted gloomily "NEPAD will never work. If the problem is an African one, what I believe is that before talking to the G-8—the very people who are responsible for the problems we have today—we should have brought it to Africa, and each country should have gathered its intellectuals and allowed them to debate it."[12] More alarming, because of his role as one of NEPAD's architects, was Senegal's President Wade's recent admonishment that NEPAD had lost direction and instead its management spends millions of dollars a year attending useless meetings that have no link with NEPAD's original goals.[13] Be that as it may, the AU has embraced NEPAD as the development model of choice.

So why has the AU enthusiastically embraced NEPAD, but not the other ECA development models before it? And more importantly, why are the BWIs not opposed to NEPAD, as they were to earlier ECA models? As shown in Chapter 2, the answer may lie in the fact that there is policy affinity between NEPAD and the neoliberal policies promoted by the World Bank and IMF.

NEPAD boasts that it "differs in its approach and strategy from all previous plans and initiatives in support of Africa's development, although the problems to be addressed remain largely the same." And it differs indeed. Some analysts see NEPAD as a self-imposed liberal reform project by the AU to appease the donor community, whose partnership and financial support NEPAD seeks. As Eddy Maloka argues:

> It is well known that the structural adjustment packages of the World Bank and IMF entailed a set of conditionalities pertaining to macroeconomic issues, public finance management and, from the late 1980's, insistence on a minimalist notion of "democracy" and compliance with the technocratic definition of "good govern-ance." For this reason, NEPAD's insistence on commitments that African leaders must first make on matters of corporate, political and economic governance is viewed as tantamount to the reintroduction of adjustment conditionalities through the back door.[14]

On the issue of accountability, one persistent criticism of NEPAD (and its review mechanism, APRM—see Box 2.1) is the lack of involve-ment by Africa's civil society in the program's design and implementa-tion. Although NEPAD makes a ritualistic appeal to the peoples of Africa, it remains fundamentally an elite-conceived program to which the African masses cannot claim ownership (see the African Civil Society Declaration, Appendix 1). Overall, it is ironic that the major elements of market and political reforms that NEPAD promotes, and which the BWIs insist on, are the very antithesis of the development path pursued by many of the Western countries during their period of industrial growth.[15]

General conclusions on African IEOs and policy development

The ECA's retreat in forging an African blueprint of self reliance and the ADB's lack of confidence in producing a development vision of its own means that in the foreseeable future NEPAD will remain the dominant framework of development in Africa. If NEPAD is a mani-festation and consolidation of the capitulation of African IEOs to the thinking of BWIs then how does one explain the ECA's cooptation and the ADB's paralysis? In order for African IEOs to become sources of competing alternatives to the mainstream economic thinking of the day, lessons ought be learned from the factors and conditions that led to the convergence in thinking by all three African IEOs to the neo-classical approach used by the World Bank and IMF in the first place. It appears two interrelated factors may help explain this puzzle.

Leadership matters

The crisis of alternative (and endogenous) development paradigms at ECA and ABD is reflected in part in the occupational backgrounds of its leadership during the era that saw the consolidation and extension of the neoliberal policies. From the late 1980s through the mid-1990s when the recommendations of the World Bank's Berg report were being implemented, the heads of the continent's African IEOs (bar NEPAD) were leaders who had not only been trained and educated in the West, but most importantly had held earlier career positions in influential roles at the World Bank or IMF. These African IEO heads were therefore not surprisingly sympathetic to the BWI policy pre-scriptions. At the ECA, the two heads (out of the seven—see Table 2.1) who have served the longest, and whose tenure has no doubt influenced the development debate the most on the continent, have been Adebayo Adedeji and Kingsley Amoako.[16] The employment backgrounds of Adedeji who championed the LPA and that of Amoako who helped craft NEPAD could not have been more different.

Adedeji, prior to joining the ECA, was a Nigerian public servant and an academic. He served as Nigeria's Federal Commissioner (Minister) for Economic Development and Reconstruction for five years (1971–75), following his tenure as a public administration professor of and director of the Institute of Administration at the University of Ife (now Obafemi Awolowo University, Ife-Ife, Nigeria). Amoako, on the other hand, prior to ECA worked in the World Bank for two decades. He was director of the Education and Social Policy Department at the World Bank and a member of the World Bank's African Strategy Review Group, which produced the Berg Report. As someone who helped draft the Berg Report it is not surprising that Amoako, prior to his appointment at the ECA in 1995, spoke and wrote about his support for the Berg Report.[17]

It is interesting to note that upon retiring from the ECA helm both Adedeji and Amoako have set up policy research centers in Africa. While Amoako's Ghana-based African Center for Economic Transformation (ACET), which aims to provide policy analysis and advisory services to African governments, receives funding from the World Bank, Adebayo's Lagos-based African Centre for Development and Strategic Studies (ACDESS), which is dedicated to multidisciplinary and strategic studies to promote development options for Africa, has received no funding support from the World Bank. The World Bank's open support for African policy research centers is designed to create and maintain a pool of sympathetic policy analysts on the continent. The observation by Richard Jolly on this phenomenon is particularly poignant. He notes:

> If we focus on Africa, I see great and specific and, I think, conscious efforts by the World Bank over the last ten or fifteen years to support research institutes in Africa and individual research workers, who all work within essentially a neo-classical World Bank paradigm of economic analysis, which, by my perspective, is excessively cautious and conservative and supportive of the international status quo. The fact that so much research money now is channeled by the World Bank to such networks—the Global Knowledge Network is one of them—and channeled to people who have matched the test of "good economics" by which is meant a rather narrow neo-classical economic paradigm, is extremely unfortunate.

Commenting on his own heterodox economic thinking, Adedeji said:

> I had to unlearn a lot of what I was taught at Harvard, London, Leicester, and Ibadan. I came to realize that development is more than mere economism, more than macroeconomic aggregates and indicators, that human beings are not mere economic beings. They are also political, social, and cultural beings as well, and these affect their behavioral patterns in the economic domain.[18]

The leadership at the ADB (Table 2.2) is more complicated since the regional members and the board of directors play a key role in the nomination and election of the president. Though there is the requirement that the president must be African, a candidate wins if they obtain a majority of the total votes cast and also a majority of the African votes. A look at the profile of the ADB presidents since the 1980s shows a line of leaders whose backgrounds were supportive of the economic thinking of the BWIs. Wila Mung'omba (1980–85) was a former IMF official, Babacar Ndiaye (1985–95) was a career employee of the ADB, and Omar Kabbaj (1995–2005) worked for both the World Bank and IMF on several African structural adjustment programs.

The leadership at NEPAD needs no examination because as already noted NEPAD is not a source of opposition to the neoliberal agenda, rather it is a manifestation of the capitulation by the ECA and ADB. As argued by 'Jìmí O. Adésìnà, NEPAD is a reflection of a class agenda that resulted from the structural adjustment of African state and civil society, not just its economies.[19] Similarly, Taylor and Nel see the authors of NEPAD as the new transnational elite of Africa who play the role of commission agents who perpetuate (perhaps unwittingly) Africa's subservient position in the global political economy.[20] Of course, there is no guarantee that the original ideas of leaders who are not seduced by the orthodox economic paradigm of the time will be adopted, as was the case with Adedeji's LPA, nor is there a guarantee that they would lead to ultimate success, as was the case with UNECLA's import substitution industrialization strategy espoused under the leadership of Raúl Prebisch. Be that as it may, the intellectual contribution of leaders of international economic institutions can have a profound influence on ideas about development paths.

Money talks

Clearly, unlike the BWIs, the ECA and ADB lack the financial resources to back up any policy ideas that they want to see implemented on the continent (see Chapter 2 for the exact budget figures for African IEOs). Lamenting on the plight of the ECA during the early 1980s, with regards to the dearth of financial resources, Adebayo Adedeji noted that "ill-digested or irrelevant ideas became beacons for policy and action because they [were] backed by resources, usually foreign."[21] He recalled further that during the debate between the LPA and Berg Report some African ministers "had received threats that their countries would be denied new loans"[22] if they openly supported the LPA over the Berg Report. As discussed in the previous chapter, economic and finance ministers in Africa play key governance role for the ECA (they meet every two years at a conference to deliberate issues for the ECA) and at the ADB (they constitute the board of governors of the Bank and meet annually to review the implementation of past policy decisions and to deliberate on new policy issues initiated by them, the board of directors or by the management of the Bank). Being cash-strapped, African governments may not want to risk going against the BWI policies for fear of losing bilateral aid, trade benefits, loans, and other forms of economic assistance. In other words the sources of funding for African governments may help explain why African IEOs have swum with the ideological currents of the day.

The evidence that the leadership in African IEOs and governments have relied a lot more on mimicry than on creativity when it comes to policymaking will not surprise scholars who analyze African development in the critical tradition.[23] Frantz Fanon's critique of the postcolonial elite is a particularly useful way of understanding this phenomenon. In his classic, *The Wretched of the Earth*, Fanon predicted that after independence Africa's national elite, empty of original ideas, would not only imitate Western economic, cultural, and political values (the cornerstone of African development today) but more importantly that Africa's leaders would act as "the the transmission line between the nation and a capitalism"[24] that keeps Africa's economies in a neocolonial state.[25] This is because the national elites, rather than seeking true development of their nations, are committed to a vision of development fundamentally limited by their class interest. In the same tradition, ECA's Adebayo Adedeji said: "Africa should not mimic the type of development that has taken place in other countries. Africa should aim to promote development that reflects its culture, politics, society and resources. It should not turn itself into a little China, a little Britain, a little America, or a little France. Development in each country or each society requires its own uniqueness."[26]

Some possible ways out

Based on the two problems presented above one can make two parallel suggestions that can improve the capacity, autonomy, and accountability of African IEOs. The first is to fund heterodox economists and social scientists in order to build a pool of leaders who ultimately may produce new ideas and make original contributions to African IEOs. The desired outcome is to articulate a counter-hegemonic discourse to the prevailing orthodox economic thinking. African governments and interested publics can provide technical and financial assistance to train policymakers (particularly economists) in non-orthodoxy. After all, the IMF and World Bank already have technical and training initiatives in place for their member countries. In addition to the IMF Institute in Washington, DC, which provides policy-oriented training for African economists, the IMF (at the prompting of African leaders, including NEPAD) in May 2002 launched the African Regional Technical Assistance Centers. The World Bank has identical programs that target African economists, including the Kenya-based African Economics Research Consortium. These training initiatives by the BWIs help perpetuate their ideological dominance. To radically rethink and reformulate alternative forms of economic knowledge, investment must be made in heterodox initiatives. One already existing initiative that could benefit from support and ultimate replication is the African Programme on Rethinking Development Economics (APORDE, see Box 3.1 for more details). There are also broadly defined social science centers that can be further harnessed. Two such centers worthy of mention are the Senegal-based Council for the Development of Social Science Research in Africa (CODESRIA) and the Ghana-based Third World Network–Africa (TRN).

One crucial reason why Africa needs an alternative non-orthodox development discourse is the neoliberal preclusion of a proactive state involvement in policymaking.[27] Historical and contemporary events, however, refute this neoliberal assumption that development will not flourish if markets are not depoliticized. As Ha-Joon Chang and others have demonstrated, rather convincingly, virtually all successful economies, both developed and developing, achieved success not through free trade and free market policies but through the selective and strategic interventions of the state in the economy.[28] The current world financial crisis and the "bail-out" responses by the industrialized countries show that a complete retreat by the state from the economic development arena, as neoliberals suggest, is utopian. This is not to suggest that the state should be excessively in charge of running markets. The call rather is for strategic state interventions in trade and

---

Box 3.1 African Programme on Rethinking Development Economics (APORDE)

Launched in 2007, and modeled on the Cambridge Programme on Rethinking Development Economics (CAPORDE), APORDE is a fully funded initiative that allows talented academics, policymakers, and civil society representatives from Africa (and, to a lesser extent, from Asia and Latin America) to gain access to alternatives to mainstream thinking on development issues and to be equipped in a way that will foster original thinking. APORDE meets annually and gives participants an intensive two-week high-level training and interaction with leading development economists. APORDE is a joint initiative of the South African Department of Trade and Industry, the French Development Agency and the French Institute of South Africa.

Source: APORDE's website, www.aporde.org.za

industrial policies. Adedeji aptly summed up the need to heterodoxy when he said "economists have to be modest about their grand universalized ideas about development. While there is a lot that developing countries can learn from the economic history of the industrialized market and non-market economies, they cannot constitute models for them."[29]

The second possibility is to create funding alternatives to options shaped by conditionality or leverage. To regain autonomy from the dictates of the BWIs' policy recommendations it is crucial that African IEOs, and perforce African governments, find alternatives to finance their projects. Financial independence from the BWIs and the donor community would give Africa the "policy space"[30] that is necessary for crafting an empowering development agenda.

But African leaders, and their IEOs, will not get the space to devise autonomous policy if they remain hooked on foreign aid.[31] It is not only because the $600 billion-plus on foreign aid to Africa since the 1960s[32] has largely been wasted, mismanaged, or misdirected, but also crucial is the fact that much of the post-Cold War aid comes largely with strings attached; conditions which compromise the economic sovereignty of African states. If policy autonomy is to become a reality then African leaders should not view foreign aid as a panacea for Africa's development woes. So far, foreign aid has created a welfare-continent mentality and has become the hub around which the spokes of most African economies turn. At the dawn of this century, more than half of African country budgets and 70 percent of their public investment came from foreign aid.[33] Fred Arkhurst described this phenomenon best when he likened Africa's dependence on foreign aid to that of an addict. He observed that "like all addictions, foreign aid has led to unexpected consequences—it has not led to development; it has not alleviated poverty, but rather has led to seemingly perpetual dependency, corruption and poverty on the part of the addicted."[34] Adebayo Adedeji concurs that dependence on foreign aid has stifled African development policy choices and exacerbated the continent's economic crisis. He observed that "because of the overly dependent nature of the Africans on external assistance, it is foreign-crafted strategies that get funded by donors and the World Bank and in such foreign-crafted strategies there is no room for the [LPA] five principles: self-reliance, self-sustainment, equity and justice, democracy and popular participation, and collective self-reliance through regional cooperation and integration."[35] This all makes the reliance of NEPAD, Africa's latest economic blueprint and institution, on foreign aid even more disturbing.

As will be discussed in Chapter 4, one of the surest ways to generate such financial revenue, and move away from its current sources of leverage, would be the expedient establishment of an AEC that unites the entire continent. Another avenue worth exploring is assistance from the African Diaspora. It is certainly a move in the right direction that the AU's Economic, Social and Cultural Council (ECOSOC) has defined the Diaspora as Africa's "sixth region." (For more on the AU and the African Diaspora, see Box 3.2.) The AU has been working on the institutional development of the African Diaspora into its organs. This is a move in the right direction toward the pan-Africanist goal of an empowered African collective at the global level. The challenge the AU faces is to clearly define the African Diaspora's rights, duties, and privileges. The African Diaspora constituency must be accorded real and tangible (and not merely symbolic) membership. If this is done it would provide an extraordinary opportunity for Africa, including African IEOs, to tap into the intellectual and material wealth of the African Diaspora for the development of the continent.

Box 3.2 The African Diaspora and the AU

The African Diaspora comprises two categories: (i) people of African heritage who "involuntarily" migrated to North America, Europe, the Caribbean, Brazil, and Latin America; and (ii) people of recent "voluntary" migration from Africa. It is estimated that over 4 million voluntary immigrants of African origin reside in the West.

The African Diaspora has played a role in the liberation and development of the continent on so many different levels. The AU, following proposals by the Senegalese government, formally incorporated the Diaspora into its organs by designating it the sixth region of Africa (the other five regions are North, South, East, West and Central Africa). In an amendment to its AU Constitutive Act, a new Article 3(q), was adopted in 3 February 2003, which declared that the AU shall "invite and encourage the full participation of the African Diaspora as an important part of our Continent, in the building of the African Union."

The debate that accompanied the amendment highlighted the need to define clearly who really is a member of the Diaspora. Some felt it should include all people of African descent and others felt that it should be restricted to only those African citizens who have gone abroad. In the end the AU executive council defined

(Box continued on next page)

the African Diaspora as: "peoples of African origin living outside the continent, irrespective of their citizenship and nationality and who are willing to contribute to the development of the continent and the building of the Africa Union." The AU has further prioritized six areas in which it hopes to engage the African Diaspora for the continent's development. They are: (i) economic cooperation, (ii) regional development and integration, (iii) women, youth and vulnerable groups, (iv) historical, socio-cultural and religious commonalities, (v) peace and security, and (vi) knowledge sharing and learning.

The AU was to hold an African and African Diaspora Summit on 7–11 October 2008 in South Africa, but that meeting was cancelled.

Source: African Union, www.africa-union.org

Conclusion

The inability of African IEOs to deal with the development challenges in Africa is all too apparent. As documented in Chapters 1 and 5, poverty remains the common lot of the majority of Africans despite nearly three decades of experimentation with neoliberalism. This disappointing record makes the continued and exclusive reliance on the policy recommendations of the BWIs an unwise choice. Further, dependence on the ideological and material resources of the BWIs betrays the lack of confidence that African IEOs have in themselves. By accepting willy-nilly, from exogenous forces, that there is only one correct path to development, African IEOs appear to be sacrificing their economic freedom. What is the point of the continent gaining its hard-won political independence only to sacrifice its economic independence at the altars of the donor community? William Easterly is correct when he observed that subservience to the ideology of BWIs is akin to the loss of freedom. He writes that "the opposite of ideology is freedom, the ability of societies to be unchained from foreign control. The only 'answer' to poverty reduction is freedom from being told the answer. Free societies and individuals are not guaranteed to succeed. They will make bad choices. But at least they bear the cost of those mistakes, and learn from them."[36] As the leading economic knowledge centers, African IEOs must exert independence in development thinking, and in the words of Frantz Fanon turn over a new leaf, and work out new concepts.[37]

4 African regional economic communities

This chapter seeks to provide a historical perspective on the evolution of African Regional Economic Communities (RECs) and to examine the challenges and strains facing these integration schemes. While all the RECs discussed were created to spur the socioeconomic transformation of the African economies, others have taken on roles that go beyond liberalization and harmonization of economic policy to include issues that address conflict resolution and regional security. After assessing the historical development and structural makeup of each REC, the chapter then explores the reasons behind the poor record of success within these institutions.

Regionalism, or RECs, come in a variety of forms and may be defined as "the adoption of a regional project by a formal regional economic organization designed to enhance the political, economic, social, cultural, and security integration and/or cooperation of member states."[1] (For REC variations and their characteristics, see Box 4.1 and Table 4.1).

In Africa, there are currently 14 such REC arrangements (for a complete list of African RECs, see Box 4.2). The main ones that will be covered in this chapter, and organized by way of age and duration, are: Economic Community of West African States (ECOWAS), Economic Community of Central African States (ECCAS), Southern African Development Community (SADC), Common Market for Eastern and Southern Africa (COMESA), Community of Sahel-Saharan States (CEN-SAD), and the East African Community (EAC). See Table 4.2 for a list of the population size and economic strength of each REC.

African regionalism in perspective

Regionalism, which has a long history in Africa, has been pursued to either enhance political unity or to foster economic growth and

Box 4.1 Classification of RECs

Preferential trade area   an arrangement in which members apply lower tariffs to imports produced by other members than to imports produced by non-members. Members can determine tariffs on imports from non-members.

Free trade area   a preferential trade area with no tariffs on imports from other members. As in preferential trade areas, members can determine tariffs on imports from non-members.

Customs union   a free trade area in which members impose common tariffs on non-members. Members may also cede sovereignty to a single customs administration.

Common market   a customs union that allows free movement of the factors of production (such as capital and labor) across national borders within the integration area.

Economic union   a common market with unified monetary and fiscal policies, including a common currency.

Political union   the ultimate stage of integration, in which members become one nation. National governments cede sovereignty over economic and social policies to a supranational authority, establishing common institutions and judicial and legislative processes—including a common parliament.

Source: El-Agara (1999).

Table 4.1 Characteristics of regional integration schemes

Scheme	Free trade among members	Common trade policy	Free factor mobility	Common monetary and fiscal policy	One government
Preferential trade area	No	No	No	No	No
Free trade area	Yes	No	No	No	No
Customs union	Yes	Yes	No	No	No
Common market	Yes	Yes	Yes	No	No
Economic union	Yes	Yes	Yes	Yes	No
Political union	Yes	Yes	Yes	Yes	Yes

Source: Ali M. El-Agara, *Regional Integration: Experience, Theory and Measurement* (1999), cited in S. K. M. Anadi, "Regional Integration in Africa: The Case of ECOWAS," D.Phil. thesis, University of Zurich, 2005.

Box 4.2 African RECs

- West African Economic and Monetary Union (UEMOA).
- Mano River Union (MRU).
- Economic Community of West African States (ECOWAS).
- Economic Community of Central African States (ECCAS).
- Central African Economic and Monetary Community (CEMAC).
- Economic Community of Great Lakes Countries (CEPGL).
- Common Market for Eastern and Southern Africa (COMESA).
- East African Community (EAC).
- Inter-Governmental Authority on Development (IGAD).
- Indian Ocean Commission (IOC).
- Southern African Development Community (SADC).
- Southern African Customs Union (SACU).
- Arab Maghreb Union (UMA).
- Community of Sahel-Saharan States (CEN-SAD).

Source: AU/ECA, *Report of the Consultative Meeting on the Rationalization of the Regional Economic Communities (RECs) for Central, North and West African Regions* (Accra, Ghana: AUC and ECA, 2005).

Table 4.2 African major Regional Economic Communities (RECs)—a snapshot

Economic institutions	Area (km²)	Population (billions)	GDP ($US billion)	GDP (per capita)	Member states
SADC	10,912,974	252,991,850	742,000	67,500	15
ECOWAS	4,189,135	133,120,686	160,808	17,300	14
ECCAS	6,667,421	137,148,620	228,256	59,300	11
COMESA	12,873,957	440,182,939	501,404	70,800	20
EAC	1,817,945	128,412,040	148,000	5,200	5
CEN-SAD	15,044,934	509,141,828	818,660	59,300	29

Source: Author compilation from *CIA World Factbook* 2008. www.cia.gov/cia/publications/factbook/

development. The Southern African Customs Union, which is recorded as the first of such experiments, was established in 1910. Other notable RECs include the Southern Rhodesia Customs Union founded in 1949 between South Africa and present-day Zimbabwe; the Ghana–Upper Volta Trade Agreement between Ghana and present-day Burkina Faso (1962); the African Common Market between Algeria, United Arab

Republic (Egypt), Ghana, Guinea, Mali, and Morocco (1962), and the East African Community, comprising Kenya, Tanzania, and Uganda (1967). Most of these earlier RECs are no longer in existence. For a sample list of failed or stillborn African REC experiments, see Table 4.3.

The impetus for regionalism has come from two main sources. The first, which originated in the immediate postcolonial era, was championed by the ECA.[2] By 1963, five years after its formation, the ECA had opened two regional offices, one in Niamey (Niger) and one in Tangier (Morocco), and was emphasizing the need for regional economic schemes, such as an African common market, the creation of an African payments union and the coordination of national development plans.[3] To facilitate the promotion of sub-regional cooperation arrangement, the ECA on 15 November 1965 signed the "Agreement of Co-operation between the Organization of African Unity and the United Nations Economic Commission for Africa." The following year, the ECA attempted (though futilely) to encourage the formation of sub-regional economic blocs, particularly ones that superseded the colonial Francophone–Anglophone linguistic divide. The ECA sponsored several successive intergovernmental meetings of all the then 14 independent West African countries in Niamey, Accra, Dakar, and Monrovia to consider the draft Articles of Association for West African Economic Cooperation prepared by the ECA secretariat.[4] In 1977, the ECA further divided Africa into five sub-regions and established offices there. These five Multinational Programming and Operational Centers (MULPOCs) were later renamed Sub-Regional Development Centers (SDCs). The ECA's proposals for the creation of RECs as building blocks that would lead to an eventual African Common Market and an African Economic Community were later adopted by the OAU conference of heads of state and government at its first economic summit in April 1980 (see Box I.1 for the AEC timeframe).[5]

Table 4.3 Sample of failed/defunct African RECs

Name	Duration
African Common Market	1962–Not implemented
Customs Union of West African States	1959–1966
Maghreb Customs Union	1960s–Not implemented
East African Common Services Organization	1961–1967
East African Community	1967–1977
East African Cooperation	1993–2000

Source: Author compilation.

Outside the ECA ambit, encouragement for regionalism in Africa has also come about, perhaps unwittingly, through another source: Africa's pre/postcolonial economic history. The former colonial structure of African economies continued to inform the continent's economic associations in the period before independence and now. This association has had a regionalist bent as the European countries sought to maintain their spheres of influence on the continent. Prior to decolonization, the four French-speaking states of Equatorial Africa—Chad, the Central African Republic, Congo (Brazzaville) and Gabon—belonged to an administrative federation called Afrique Equatoriale Française (AEF). The AEF was created by a French decree of the 15 January 1910, and helped lay the foundations for future Francophone economic relations in Africa.[6] Furthermore, the treaty establishing the European Economic Community (EEC) that was signed in Rome on 25 March 1957 by the representatives of the Federal Republic of Germany, Belgium, France, Italy, Luxembourg and the Netherlands, further created a "special relationship" between the African colonies and the "Community of Six." When the Treaty of Rome entered into force on 1 January 1958, the overseas countries and territories to which the provisions of Part IV of the treaty applied included all African dependencies and 17 Francophone countries in particular. The terms of association embodied in Part IV of the EEC treaty, which was to operate for five years, provided that the exports of associate countries could enter the markets of the Community of Six duty-free and that associate countries could even protect their industries, at the expense of the Community of Six, if they so chose. Writing on the general incentives provided for associate countries, Tom Soper observed that

> there is no doubt that these provisions gave considerable benefits to the associates. They would have duty free access to a dynamic European market of 170 million people; they were not prevented from protecting their economies, and they were the beneficiaries of a Development Fund of some size, and one which was over and above any bilateral aid they were already receiving."[7]

The march to statehood by most of the Rome Treaty associates in the early 1960s necessitated a new relationship between the Community of Six and their former colonies. This new relationship was institutionalized at the Yaoundé Convention for the periods 1964–69 and 1970–75 respectively.

So quite early on we see that the special relationship of European Community (EC) and the various groups of associates demonstrate the significance of the regionalism in Africa's development.[8] The accession of Great Britain to the EC in 1973 further necessitated the need to rearrange the economic relationship between the EC and their former colonies. This led to the first Lomé convention of 1975 that included economic agreement with the EC and African states as well as a number of Commonwealth, Caribbean, and Pacific countries (ACP).[9] Between 1975 and 2000 there were four Lomé conventions. Some of features of these conventions include: the granting of free access on a basis of non-reciprocity for most of the ACP exports to the EC, the introduction of a system for the stabilization of export earnings (STABEX) for 12 major ACP commodities (under Lomé 1); and the introduction of the SYSMIN mechanism to stabilize export earnings from minerals (under Lomé II).

The successor to the Lomé Coventions, the Cotonou Agreement and the Economic Partnership Agreements (EPAs), which currently define the economic relationships between EU and the ACP countries further, affirms regionalism as a strategy for development.[10] The essence this strategy is captured in the 1997 EU Green Paper on Development Cooperation:

> Regional integration among developing countries is part of a wider strategy to promote equitable growth and is not an end in itself. Effective regional integration will increase competition, reduce private transaction costs, enable firms to exploit economies of scale, encourage inward foreign investment and facilitate macro-economic policy coordination. Regional groupings should be open towards the world market in the sense of keeping tariffs at a level that does not encourage trade diversion. They should not attempt a form of regional autarky that has led to past failures. Open regionalism complements unilateral liberalization. Without regional coherence, unilateral liberalization may imply negative spill-over effects. A regionally coherent liberalization strategy will reduce and smoothen the cost of adjustment to an economy in the face of globalization, both for the private and public sector. The high adjustment cost of unilateral liberalization has been a cause of policy reversal in a number of developing economies.[11]

The EU's insistence, under the EPAs, that trade relations be negotiated with ACP countries engaged in a regional integration process, and not with individual states (except in exceptional circumstances) demonstrates that regionalism would continue to be part of the institutional puzzle for Africa's development.

ECOWAS

The Economic Community of West African States (ECOWAS), also known as La Communauté Economique Des Etats de l'Afrique de l'Ouest (CEDEAO) is one of the oldest thriving RECs in Africa. It was established by the Treaty of Lagos on 28 May 1975[12] by 15 West African countries with the mission to promote trade, economic integration and self-reliance in West Africa. The current ECOWAS members are: Benin, Burkina Faso, Cape Verde, Côte d'Ivoire, Gambia, Ghana, Guinea, Guinea-Bissau, Liberia, Mali, Niger, Nigeria, Senegal, Sierra Leone, and Togo (Cape Verde joined ECOWAS in 1976, and Mauritania withdrew its membership in December 2000, having announced its intention to do so in December 1999). Article 2(1) of the 1975 treaty described the objectives of ECOWAS as follows:

> to promote co-operation and development in all fields of economic activity particularly in the fields of industry, transport, telecommunications, energy, agriculture, natural resources, commerce, monetary and financial questions and in social and cultural matters for the purpose of raising the standard of living of its peoples, of increasing and maintaining economic stability, of fostering closer relations among its members and of contributing to the progress and development of the African continent.

Article2(2) of this treaty lays out the stages for the attainment of these objectives. It calls for the elimination of customs duties between the member states, the abolition of quantitative and administrative restrictions on trade, the establishment of a common customs tariff and a common commercial policy toward third countries, the abolition of the obstacles to the free movement of persons, services and capital between the member states, the harmonization of the agricultural policies and the promotion of common projects (notably in the fields of marketing, research, and Afro-industrial enterprises), and the implementation of schemes for the joint development of transport, communication, energy, and the infrastructural facilities, as well as the harmonization of the economic and industrial policies.

The fundamental principles of ECOWAS are: equality of member states, solidarity and collective self-reliance, interstate cooperation, harmonization of policies and integration of programs, nonaggression between member states, and maintenance of regional peace, stability and security through the promotion and strengthening of good neighborliness. To carry out its aims the treaty called for the creation of the three major institutions (the Authority of Heads of State and Government, the Council of Ministers, and the Executive Secretariat). It also called for the establishment of four technical and specialized commissions in the areas of: trade customs, immigration, monetary and payments; industry, agriculture and natural resources; transport, telecommunications and energy; and social and cultural affairs.

The 1975 treaty had aimed for the establishment of a common market in 15 years, but this did not materialize (see discussion below on problems with RECs). Reflecting on ECOWAS' failings, Abbas Bundu, the secretary of ECOWAS, confessed in 1991 that in its first 15 years (1975–90) "politically nothing was done to apply the laws and decisions of the Community."[13] In a bid to accelerate the pace of economic integration and political cooperation, ECOWAS members have made several significant restructurings of the 1975 treaty. On 24 July 1993, for instance, ECOWAS revised the original treaty by creating new goals such as the creation of a common economic market and a single currency, establishing new institutions and consolidating others.

As a result of this restructuring ECOWAS is now made up of the Authority of Heads of State and Government, which is the supreme decision making organ of the Community. This body meets once a year, with a rotational chairperson drawn from the member states (see Table 4.4 for a list of the chairpersons to date). There is also the Council of Ministers which consists of two representatives from each member country. It meets twice a year, and is responsible for the running of the Community.

As noted earlier, ECOWAS has created new institutions and consolidated others. For example, a 120-member ECOWAS Parliament, based in Abuja, Nigeria, was inaugurated in November 2000. (Following institutional reforms in January 2006, however, the number of parliamentarians was reduced from 120 to 115.) ECOWAS, in January 2001, crossed another milestone when it established a Court of Justice made up of seven judges who serve five-year renewable terms. Another new institution, the ECOWAS Bank for Investment and Development (EBID) commenced operations on 1 January 2004.[14] EBID has two subsidiaries, namely: the ECOWAS Regional Development Fund (ERDF) which focuses on public sector financing, and the ECOWAS Regional Investment Bank (ERIB) which is dedicated to private sector financing.

Examples of consolidated institutions include the West African Health Organization (WAHO). WAHO became operational in March 2000 following the merger of the West African Health Community (founded

Table 4.4 ECOWAS chairpersons

Name	Country	Tenure
Gnassingbé Eyadéma	Togo	1977–1978
Olusegun Obasanjo	Nigeria	1978–1979
Léopold Sédar Senghor	Senegal	1979–1980
Gnassingbé Eyadéma	Togo	1980–1981
Siaka Stevens	Sierra Leone	1981–1982
Mathieu Kérékou	Benin	1982–1983
Ahmed Sékou Touré	Guinea	1983–1984
Lansana Conté	Guinea	1984–1985
Muhammadu Buhari	Nigeria	1985–27 Aug. 1985
Ibrahim Babangida	Nigeria	27 Aug. 1985–1989
Dawda Jawara	Gambia	1989–1990
Blaise Compaoré	Burkina Faso	1990–1991
Dawda Jawara	Gambia	1991–1992
Abdou Diouf	Senegal	1992–1993
Nicéphore Soglo	Benin	1993–1994
Jerry John Rawlings	Ghana	1994–27 July 1996
Sani Abacha	Nigeria	27 July 1996–8 June 1998
Abdulsalami Abubakar	Nigeria	9 June 1998–1999
Gnassingbé Eyadéma	Togo	1999
Alpha Oumar Konaré	Mali	1999–21 Dec. 2001
Abdoulaye Wade	Senegal	21 Dec. 2001–31 Jan. 2003
John Agyekum Kufuor	Ghana	31 Jan. 2003–19 Jan. 2005
Mamadou Tandja	Niger	19 Jan. 2005–Present

Source: Author compilation from various reports.

in 1978) and the Organization for Co-ordination and Co-operation in the Struggle against Endemic Diseases (founded in 1960). As the sub-region's leading health institution, WAHO aims to harmonize health policies, promote research and disseminate information for ECOWAS members.

ECOWAS currently has eight technical commissions, comprising representatives of each member state. The technical commissions cover diverse areas such as food and agriculture, and administration and finance. The ECOWAS Economic and Social Council is yet to be formally institutionalized.

The main administrative arm of ECOWAS, the Executive Secretariat (now the ECOWAS Commission) has similarly been transformed. This followed an agreement by heads of state of its member countries at a one-day summit held in Niamey, Niger, on 12 January 2005, who maintained that the transformation was necessary, as it would help the Commission focus better on the discharge of its core function. The transformation from Secretariat to Commission took place in January 2007 with election of a nine-member commission headed by a president. The Commission is elected for a four-year term, renewable once (see Table 4.5 for a list of the heads of the Secretariat). As of 2006, the Commission had a US$121 million operational budget.

To achieve the objectives of establishing a common market and the creation of a monetary union, the ECOWAS Monetary Cooperation Program (EMCP) requires member countries to undertake economic reforms to achieve some common economic targets known as convergence criteria. The goal is complicated since the Francophone countries in ECOWAS already have in existence a West African Monetary Union (UEMOA), which they regard as superior. To circumvent this problem, Nigeria and Ghana (Anglophone countries), proposed a fast track to monetary integration for ECOWAS member countries. This initiative led to the establishment of the West African Monetary Zone (WAMZ) as the second monetary zone in the ECOWAS, on 15 December 2000. The major objective is to facilitate the rapid achievement of a WAMZ monetary union with a common central bank and a single currency for eventual merger with the UEMOA under the ECOWAS. The requirements under the EMCP convergence criteria include: a single-digit inflation of less than 5 percent, budget deficit to gross domestic product (GDP) ratio of less than 4 percent, central bank financing of government budget limited to 10 percent of previous year's tax revenue, and gross external reserves should finance not less than three months' import cover. Other secondary criteria are the prohibition of new domestic debt arrears and liquidation of existing ones; tax revenue to GDP, wage bill/tax revenue and public investment/ tax revenue should not be less than 20, 35 and 20 percent respectively; maintaining real exchange and interest rates. ECOWAS has reaffirmed the introduction of a second WAMZ (scheduled for 2009) and has

Table 4.5 ECOWAS executive secretaries

Name	Country	Tenure
Aboubakar Diaby Ouattara	Côte d'Ivoire	Jan. 1977–1985
Momodu Munu	Sierra Leone	1985–1989
Abass Bundu	Sierra Leone	1989–1993
Édouard Benjamin	Guinea	1993–1997
Lansana Kouyaté	Guinea	Sept. 1997–31 Jan. 2002
Mohamed Ibn Chambas	Ghana	1 Feb. 2002–Present

Source: ECOWAS Secretariat, www.ecowas.int

called on member states to comply with the macroeconomic convergence criteria.

ECOWAS has also urged members to adhere to the full implementation of the Protocol on Free Movement of Persons, the Right of Residence and Establishment. At its 23rd session in May 2000, the ECOWAS heads launched an ECOWAS passport. National passports are to be phased out in five years in countries where the ECOWAS passport is introduced. However, as of October 2007, only six member countries (Liberia, Benin, Senegal, Nigeria, Niger, and Ghana) were using the ECOWAS passport. An ECOWAS travel certificate, which is valid for two years from the date of issue, is also in place.

Though it is an economic bloc, ECOWAS has taken on issues dealing with conflict resolution and security within its region. One of the transformative initiatives undertaken by ECOWAS since its inception has been its attempt, through ECOMOG (ECOWAS Monitoring Group), to resolve the region's conflicts (see Box 4.3).

Economic Community of Central African States (ECCAS)

ECCAS was established on 18 October 1983 by the member states of the Central African Customs and Economic Union (UDEAC) and the members of the Economic Community of the Great Lakes States (CEPGL) (Burundi, Rwanda and the then Zaire) as well as Sao Tomé and Principe. The ten current members are: Angola, Burundi, Cameroon, Central Africa, Chad, Gabon, Congo, Democratic Republic of Congo, Equatorial Guinea, and São Tomé and Principe. Rwanda withdrew its membership in June 2007. ECCAS became operational in 1985 and aims to achieve collective regional autonomy, raise the standard of living of its populations and maintain economic stability through harmonious cooperation. Its ultimate goal is to establish a Central African Common Market over a period of 12 years.[15]

Article 4(2) of the Treaty Establishing the Economic Community of Central African States lays out the objectives for the organization. These include: the elimination between member states of customs duties and any other charges having an equivalent effect levied on imports and exports, the abolition between member states of quantitative restrictions and other trade barriers, the establishment and maintenance of an external common customs tariff, the establishment of a trade policy vis-à-vis third states, the progressive abolition between member states of obstacles to the free movement of persons, goods, services and capital and to the right of establishment, and the harmonization of national policies in order to promote community activities,

Box 4.3 ECOMOG

The ECOWAS Monitoring Group or ECOMOG is an ad hoc military force consisting of land, sea, and air units that was established by ECOWAS to deal with the humanitarian and security crisis that ensued during the civil war in Liberia in 1990.

In the midst of anarchy and chaos and with his political survival on the line, Liberia's President Doe wrote a letter, dated 14 July 1990, to the ECOWAS Standing Mediation Committee and implored his fellow ECOWAS leaders to act. President Doe's letter stated, among things:

> in order to avert the wanton destruction of lives and properties and further forestall the reign of terror, I wish to call on your Honorable Body to take note of my personal concerns and the collective wishes of the people of Liberia, and to assist in finding a constitutional and reasonable solution to the crisis in our country as early as possible. Particularly it would seem most expedient at this time to introduce an ECOWAS Peacekeeping Force into Liberia to forestall increasing terror and tension and to assure a peaceful transitional environment.[1]

It is instructive to note that though ECOWAS was created solely as an REC its members adopted two important defense protocols in 1978 and 1981. These protocols called for mutual respect and non-interference in the domestic affairs of member states and the establishment of a regional mechanism for mutual assistance in defense matters. At the same time the defense protocols called for member states to intervene in the "internal armed conflict within any Member State engineered and supported actively from outside likely to endanger the security and peace in the entire Community." This clause, which is enshrined in the 1981 Protocol on Mutual Defense Assistance, also provided for the establishment of an Allied Armed Force of the Community (AAFC) as needed.

It is against this backdrop that the ECOWAS Standing Mediation Committee in a meeting in Banjul, Gambia, on 7 August 1990, took the decision to send a military force to intervene in the conflict in Liberia. ECOMOG forces (led by Nigeria) moved into Liberia to

(*Box continued on next page*)

restore peace on 25 August 1990, the first African REC to deploy military forces into another member state's territory. The ECOMOG force was initially made up of some 4,000 troops from Nigeria, Ghana, Guinea, Sierra Leone, and Gambia. ECOMOG's core functions are threefold:

- combat intervention, which involves the deployment of ECOMOG at the request of a legally constituted government to prevent an internal situation from degenerating into anarchy;
- peace enforcement, which involves the use of diplomacy and the threat of force to get armed factions to the reach negotiated settlement, and may also include monitoring and enforcing a ceasefire;
- peacekeeping activities, which include humanitarian operations and providing security for prisoners of war.

ECOMOG operates under directives from the heads of state of ECOWAS members, and the day-to-day issues and political directives are handled by the ECOWAS Secretariat.

To date ECOMOG has since been involved in five major conflict resolution situations: Liberia (1990–99), Sierra Leone (1997–2000), Guinea-Bissau (1998–99), Guinea (2001), and Côte d'Ivoire (2003–present).[2]

Notes:
1 The full text of President Doe's letter is reprinted in Marc Weller, ed., *Regional Peacekeeping and International Enforcement: The Liberian Crisis* (Cambridge University Press, 1994), 60.
2 For additional reading on ECOMOG, see the South African-based Institute for Security Studies paper, "The Evolution and Conduct of ECOMOG Operations in West Africa": http://www.iss.co.za/Pubs/Monographs/No44/ECOMOG.html. Also see Human Rights Watch, "Waging War to Keep the Peace: The ECOMOG Intervention and Human Rights," www.hrw.org/reports/1993/liberia.

particularly in industry, transport and communications, energy, agriculture, natural resources, trade, currency and finance, human resources, tourism, education, culture, science, and technology;

At a heads of state conference in 1999, ECCAS identified four priority fields for the organization: to develop capacities to maintain peace, security, and stability, which are essential prerequisites for economic and social development; to develop physical, economic, and monetary integration; to develop a culture of human integration; and to establish an autonomous financing mechanism for ECCAS. Toward the goal of promoting and maintaining peace and security in the region, ECCAS created the Council for Peace and Security in Central Africa (COPAX). COPAX has three units: the Central African Early-Warning System (MARAC) collects and analyzes data for the early detection and prevention of crises. The second division, the Defense and Security Commission (CDS), is a meeting of chiefs of staff of national armies and commanders-in-chief of police and gendarmerie forces from the different member states to plan, organize, and provide advice to the decision making bodies of the community in order to initiate military operations if needed. The final unit of COPAX is the Central African Multinational Force (FOMAC). It is a non-permanent force consisting of military contingents from member states, whose purpose is to accomplish missions of peace, security, and humanitarian relief.

The protocol establishing COPAX entered into force in June 2002. As of this writing, ECCAS (prompted by Angola) was undergoing restructuring in order to make it a more efficient and dynamic body, including the clarification of the mandates of the rotational presidency and secretariat.

ECCAS is composed of a: Conference of Heads of State and Government; Council of Ministers; General Secretariat (one secretary-general elected for four years and three assistant secretaries-general); Court of Justice; and a Consultative Commission.

Southern African Development Community (SADC)

The forerunner of the Southern African Development Community (SADC) was the Southern African Development Coordination Conference (SADCC). SADCC emerged from the activities of the Front Line States (Angola, Botswana, Mozambique, Tanzania and Zambia), which as an ad hoc OAU Summit Committee, worked for the support and liberation of Zimbabwe and Namibia and for the ending of apartheid in South Africa. When Zimbabwe gained her independence in 1980, the Front Line States focused their attention on the political situation in Namibia and apartheid and, "especially, the economic position of the independent states vis-à-vis South Africa itself." It is within this context that SADCC was formed in Lusaka, Zambia, on 1 April 1980, following the adoption of the Lusaka Declaration, which was titled *Southern Africa: Towards Economic Liberation*. The nine founding member states of SADCC were Angola, Botswana, Lesotho,

Malawi, Mozambique, Swaziland, Tanzania, Zambia, and Zimbabwe. The four principal objectives were: the reduction of economic dependence, particularly, but not only, on the Republic of South Africa; the forging of links to create a genuine and equitable regional integration; the mobilization of resources to promote the implementation of national interstate and regional policies; and taking concerted action to secure international cooperation within the framework of its strategy for economic liberation.

SADCC clearly sought autonomy in its trade relations with apartheid South Africa and to adopt influential policies for the entire Southern Africa region. However, a complete break with South Africa's economic stranglehold proved a dilemma for SADDC since most of the member states were heavily dependent on South Africa's economy for survival. The fact is, apart from Tanzania, all the Front Line States were heavily dependent on South Africa in terms of trade, industry, and transportation for their imports and exports. Botswana, Lesotho, Swaziland and Namibia, for example, were members of SACU (Southern African Customs Union), which was headed and controlled by South Africa. Similarly, Zimbabwe, Mozambique, and Malawi were all bound by trade agreements with the apartheid regime. Though Zambia had no formal agreements with South Africa, its mining industry was heavily dependent on the South Africa economy. Thus SADCC's quest for economic autonomy from South Africa did not seem plausible. As former SADCC chairman, President Quett Masire, observed: "It is difficult for us to be seen championing the cause of sanctions against South Africa when in fact it is going to hurt us before it hurts South Africa."[16]

The treaty establishing SADC, which replaced SADCC, was signed at the summit of heads of state or government on 17 August 1992, in Windhoek, Namibia. The SADCC leaders felt a need to transform the Coordination Conference (SADDC) to a Development Community (SADC) in order to create a more institutionalized legal structure with more formal status, one that could speed up the harmonization and integration of the member states' economies to ensure collective self-reliance and overall regional development. It is instructive to note that the transformation from SADDC to SADC came in the wake of apartheid's demise. Among other things, the summit expressed the hope that a democratic South Africa will join the SADC family of nations.

SADC exists to: achieve development and economic growth; evolve common political values, systems and institutions; promote and defend peace and security; promote self-sustaining development on the basis of collective self-reliance, and the interdependence of member states;

achieve complementarity between national and regional strategies and programs; promote and maximize productive employment and utilization of resources of the region; and to strengthen and consolidate the long-standing historical, social and cultural affinities and links among the people of the region.[17]

Four years after SADC's founding, and with the horrors of apartheid still fresh in their minds, the leaders of SADC decided to create a protocol on Politics, Defense and Security. This was contained in a communiqué of the SADC heads of state meeting in Gaborone, Botswana, on 28 June 1996. The SADC Organ of Politics, Defense and Security specifies a number of objectives which, inter alia, include the following: to promote political cooperation among member states and evolution of common political value systems and institutions; to mediate in interstate and intra-state disputes and conflicts; to develop close cooperation between the police and security services of the region, with a view to addressing cross-border crime, as well as promoting a community-based approach on matters of security; to promote and enhance the development of democratic institutions and practices within member states and to encourage the observance of universal human rights as provided for in the charters and conventions of the OAU and the United Nations; and to develop a collective security capacity and conclude a mutual defense pact for responding to external threats, and a regional peacekeeping capacity within national armies that could be called upon within the region or elsewhere on the continent.

There were, however, disagreements within SADC regarding the future status and operations of the organ, either as an integrated part of the SADC (favored by South Africa) or as a more autonomous body (supported by Zimbabwe). In the end, proposals to establish the Organ for Politics, Defense and Security as a substructure of SADC, with subdivisions for defense and international diplomacy, to be chaired by a member country's head of state, working within a troika system, was approved.

SADC's current member states are Angola, Botswana, Democratic Republic of Congo, Lesotho, Madagascar, Malawi, Mauritius, Mozambique, Namibia, Seychelles,[18] South Africa, Swaziland, Tanzania, Zambia, and Zimbabwe.

There are four principal institutions of SADC. First, there is the Summit, which is comprised of heads of state and/or government and is responsible for the general policy direction and programming of the SADC. Next, is the Council of Ministers, which consists of ministers from each member state (usually from the ministries of foreign affairs and economic planning or finance). Then there is the Integrated Committee of Ministers, which exists to ensure policy guidance, coordination and harmonization of cross sector activities. It is made up of at least two ministers from each member state responsible to the Council of Ministers. Meetings of the Summit and the Integrated Committee of Ministers take place annually, while the Council of Ministers meets biannually (in February to approve the annual budgets and in August to prepare the summit agenda). The final major body of SADC is the Secretariat. Headquartered in Gaborone, Botswana, the Secretariat is responsible for handling the day to day planning, coordination and management of the organization's programs. It is headed by an executive secretary who is appointed by the Summit. SADC's administrative budget for 2007 was US$8.9 million.

One unique feature of SADC is its troika system. The SADC troika system vests authority in the incumbent chairperson, incoming chairperson who is the deputy chairperson at the time and the immediate previous chairperson. The troika system was established in August 1999 to help SADC execute its tasks and decisions in an expeditious manner. The troika system runs through the structures of SADC at Summit, Council of Ministers, and senior officials at the Secretariat. The format also applies to the Organ on Politics, Defense and Security.

SADC officially launched a Free Trade Area (FTA) at its August 2008 summit under the theme "SADC Free Trade Area for Growth, Development and Wealth Creation." The introduction of the FTA is geared to the establishment of a customs union by 2010, a common market by 2015, and a monetary union by 2016. At this same summit, gender activists secured the signing of a "long delayed gender protocol" that calls for "fifty per cent representation by women at all levels of government by 2015 and further calls for member states to put in place legislative measures which guarantee that political and policy structures are gender sensitive."[19] SADC has also endorsed the establishment of the SADC Regional Development Fund to finance development projects, and representatives of the private sector in SADC have established the Association of SADC Chambers of Commerce, based in Mauritius.

Common Market for Eastern and Southern Africa (COMESA)

COMESA began operations in December 1994 when it replaced the former Preferential Trade Area (PTA) for Eastern and Southern Africa, which had existed since 1981. COMESA's member countries are Angola, Burundi, Comoros, Congo, Djibouti, Egypt, Eritrea, Ethiopia, Kenya, Libya, Madagascar, Malawi, Mauritius, Rwanda, Seychelles, Sudan, Swaziland, Uganda, Zambia, and Zimbabwe. Former members include: Lesotho (quit in 1997), Mozambique (quit in 1997), Tanzania (quit in September 2000), and Namibia (quit in May 2004).

The specific objectives establishing COMESA include: promoting sustainable growth of the member states, promoting joint development in all fields of economic activity and harmonization of macroeconomic policies, creating an enabling environment for foreign, cross-border, and domestic investment, and establishing peace, security, and stability among the member states.

COMESA has seven major organs. They are: the Authority, which is composed of heads of states or government. As the supreme policy organ of COMESA, the Authority is responsible for the general policy and direction and control of the performance of the executive functions of the institution. The Council of Ministers is made up of government appointed ministers who meet once a year and is responsible for general policymaking. There is a Court of Justice, which as the legal arm ensures the adherence to law in the interpretation and application of the Treaty and is composed of seven judges. The Court of Justice became operational in September 1998. The Committee of Governors of Central Banks advises the Authority and the Council of Ministers on monetary and financial issues and is responsible for enhancing the fiscal and monetary union of COMESA. Next is the Intergovernmental Committee of Permanent or Principal Secretaries designated by each member state and responsible for the development of strategy in all portfolios except economics and finance. There are also 12 technical committees that handle: Administrative and Budgetary Matters, Agriculture, Comprehensive Information Systems, Energy, Finance and Monetary Affairs, Industry, Labor, Human Resources and Social Affairs, Legal Affairs, Natural Resources and Environment, Tourism and Wildlife, Trade and Customs, and Transport and Communications. COMESA's Secretariat, which is responsible for overall coordination is based in Lusaka, Zambia.

In October 2000, COMESA launched its FTA, making it the first FTA in Africa. COMESA hopes to launch its customs union in December 2008. It has also endorsed the creation of monetary institute to prepare the zone for the future monetary union and the creation of the COMESA fund to support infrastructure development in the zone. Though COMESA has been a free trade area since 2000, as of this writing only 13 of its 20 members had signed on to the FTA pact.

The Community of Sahel-Saharan States (CEN-SAD)

Formerly known as COMESSA, CEN-SAD was established on 4 February 1998 by six countries (Burkina Faso, Chad, Libya, Mali, Niger, and Sudan) but since then its membership has grown to 29, making it Africa's largest trade bloc. One of its main goals is to achieve economic unity through the creation of a free trade area for its member states, which span Western, Northern and Central Africa. The objectives of CEN-SAD are the establishment of a global economic union based on the implementation of a community development plan that complements the local development plans of member states and which comprises the various fields of a sustained socioeconomic development. Additionally, CEN-SAD seeks the adoption of necessary measures to ensure the free movement of persons and capital, and the increased integration of policy among its members.

The major institutions of CEN-SAD are the Conference of Leaders and Heads of State, the Executive Council, the General Secretariat, the Sahel-Saharan Investment and Trade Bank, and the Economic, Social and Cultural Council (ESCC). CEN-SAD is based in the Libyan capital, Tripoli.

At a meeting of the Summit in Tripoli, in June 2006, the chairman of CEN-SAD was charged with the task of working toward the merging of CEN-SAD, the Arab Maghreb Union (AMU), and ECOWAS, in order to accelerate the creation of the African Economic Community. Much of the funding for CEN-SAD is rumored to come from Libya's leader, Muammar Al Qathafi.

The East African Community (EAC)

The EAC is the latest postcolonial regional experiment for East African states since the collapse of the East African Common Services Organization (1961–67), the East African Community (1967–77), and the East African Cooperation (1993–2000). For a list of failed African REC experiments, see Table 4.3.

The treaty establishing the East African Community was signed on 30 November 1999 and entered into force on 7 July 2000 following its ratification by the three founding member states—Kenya, Uganda, and Tanzania. Rwanda and Burundi later acceded to the EAC Treaty on 18 June 2007 and became full members of EAC on 1 July 2007. Like the other RECs, the EAC envisages the eventual unification of political, economic and social policies. The specific objectives of the treaty are to: promote sustainable growth and equitable development of partner states, to strengthen and consolidating the long-standing political, economic, social, cultural, and traditional ties by partner states, to enhance the participation of the private sector and civil society in regional development, to mainstream gender in all its programs and enhancement of the role of women in development, and to promote good governance, peace, and stability within the region.

The structure of EAC consists of six principal organs. The Summit is made up of heads of government of member states. The Council of Ministers, which is the main decision making institution, is made up of ministers from member states responsible for regional cooperation. The third and fourth organs are the Coordinating Committee, which consists of permanent secretaries, and the Sectoral Committees. The ECA also boasts of a Court of Justice a 27-member East African Legislative Assembly. The final organ, the EAC Secretariat, which serves as the executive organ of the institution, is headquartered in Arusha, Tanzania.

The EAC has approved the establishment of a customs union, and extended preferential tariff treatment for goods originating from COMESA and SADC countries until the end of 2008. It has also endorsed the cooperation between EAC, COMESA and SADC in harmonizing their policies and programs. The EAC has also begun issuing common passports and made its members' currencies convertible.

Appraisal and challenges of African RECs

African RECs face a number of pressing difficulties and weaknesses that hamper their overall success. The following is a discussion of related problems that Africa's RECs face. To begin with, African RECS face a myriad of enforcement problems. As has been stated earlier, the highest authority of African RECs are the heads of government. The absence of strong supranational institutions to ensure strict compliance, and the lack of enforcement mechanisms to sanction refractory or noncompliant states makes it difficult to implement trade liberalization and other integration measures. Indeed, the difficulty in implementing REC treaties is the most widely cited obstacle to integration, as states can willy-nilly flaunt protocols and treaties they are signatories to without fear of facing punitive measures. In most cases, the absence of monitoring schemes and the domestication of treaties slow down integration efforts, since agreed timetables and macroeconomic targets, on such matters as reducing tariffs and nontariff barriers, are missed by wide margins.

The sheer number of RECs has also created problems because of overlapping membership. More than half of Africa's 53 countries belong to two or more RECs; with just five countries maintaining membership in one REC. A majority of African countries cite political and strategic reasons as main factors for joining an REC. Economic and geographic calculations are not the major factors cited.[20] The scholarship on the impact of multiple REC membership tends to be mixed. There are those who view multiple REC memberships as beneficial for regional integration. They contend that membership in several RECs can speed up the process of integration and minimize the potential losses associated with single REC membership. On the other hand, there are those who argue that since most African RECs have similar objectives, multiplicity of membership leads to wasteful duplication of functions. RECs in this context are seen as stumbling blocks, rather than building blocks, to the ultimate goal of a pan-African economic union. It is hard to dismiss the argument of the latter. For example, how practical is the envisioned free trade area of CEN-SAD when it overlaps with the envisioned customs unions of ECOWAS, ECCAS, and COMESA and other trade blocs more advanced in their integration? Warning of the pitfalls that occur with multiple REC membership, the ECA notes that

> a country belonging to two or more regional economic communities not only faces multiple financial obligations, but must cope with different meetings, policy decisions, instruments, procedures, and schedules. Customs officials have to deal with different tariff reduction rates, rules of origin, trade documentation, and statistical nomenclatures. The range of requirements multiplies customs procedures and paperwork, counter to trade liberalization's goals of facilitating and simplifying trade.[21]

Most African RECs are mindful of the challenges posed by overlapping memberships and have began taking measures to avoid duplication of efforts. SADC and COMESA for example established a joint task force in 2001 to deal with common issues.

Multiple REC membership also creates compensation problems for these organizations. Because member countries remain at different levels of development with regard to each REC objective, they most often times attach different degrees of importance to each objective. Weak and strong economies alike make strategic calculations on the gains and benefits of integration. To garner strong loyalty to REC affiliation there ought to be some form of compensation mechanism for the losers in the integration process. Perhaps the lack of a compensation arrangement explains why some many African countries have multiple memberships.

This also suggests another issue for RECs: the developing nature of many African member states leads to infrastructural and economic resource problems. The general infrastructure in Africa, be it in areas of technology or transportation networks, is very weak. This makes the physical integration of the continent particularly difficult. It does not help that intra-REC trade, perhaps due to the similarity of exports, is extremely low. For example, only 4 percent of the export trade is between SADC members. This problem is compounded by the fact that the continent has a fragile, in some cases unstable, macroeconomic and financial environment. As the ECA noted, most African RECs have "significant differences in tariffs, inflation, exchange rates, debt-to-GDP ratios, rate of money growth and other vital macroeconomic variables between member countries."[22] The vulnerability of economic climate is further exacerbated by the inconvertibility of currencies among African RECs, scarcity of foreign exchange and the high cost of imported capital goods from the industrialized countries. It must also be quickly added that most of the RECs are cash-strapped because financial contributions are not forthcoming or consistent. The ECA has further noted, for example, that

> as member countries have expanded the mandate of the regional economic communities, they have not increased funding. And member countries are frequently late in paying their assessed contributions. The most visible consequence of these funding problems is the weak staffing situation in the secretariats and the consequent lack of programmatic visibility.[23]

For instance, ECCAS began functioning in 1985, but was inactive for several years because of financial difficulties (non-payment of membership fees). One can argue that the lack of financial resources makes the multiplicity of membership in RECs especially problematic.

A study of Ghana's trading relationship with other ECOWAS nations accurately captures the many problems already cited. The CTA's conclusion is that,

> a wide range of barriers makes even this low level of regional trade difficult to achieve and frequently uncompetitive. Market knowledge is inadequate and accurate tariff and technical data is hard to obtain. Trade finance is poorly developed and expensive. Language differences, harassment at borders and roadblocks discourage many entrepreneurs and add to the costs. The ECOWAS Secretariat has few powers to force governments to implement trade liberalization measures. Ten different currencies are in use, but most are not accepted in international trade, and the West African Clearing House is unable to prevent serious delays in settling payments between some member states.[24]

Furthermore, most African leaders pay lip service to the idea of regionalism without having the will or desire to subordinate their national economic and political sovereignty to regional objectives. This usually leads to the failure by REC members to enact national regulations to mirror integration protocols, a slow (and often times lengthy) protocol ratification and implementation process, and an unevenness in compliance with regional arrangements. Numerous reasons are cited for the lack of political commitment to RECs. Some stress the divergent ideologies and class interests of member states while others emphasize the cost-benefit calculations by members on regionalism.[25] Still others argue that the real culprit is the lack of Weberian governance structures in Africa. As seen by Ominiyi Adewoye,

> a system of governance that is devoid of defined mechanisms and structures of representation or participation undermines the kind of consistent political commitment and long-term legitimacy that regional integration demands, because a change of ruler is sufficient to undermine agreements arrived at by his predecessor. Concentration of power also makes it difficult to promote healthy inter-governmental relations other than the very top.[26]

Be that as it may, the fact remains that members of African RECs have done little to ratify and domesticate the treaties they have signed. A case in point is that ECOWAS during its 33 years of existence has adopted over 52 conventions and protocols but its member states have ratified only 36. Non-ratification, and a retreat to sovereignty claims, becomes more prevalent when it involves protocols bordering on security issues. In the case of ECOWAS, all member states had ratified the Protocol on Free Movement of Persons, Residence and Establishment by 2008, but only 6 of its 15 members had ratified the protocol relating to Conflict Prevention, Management, Resolution and Security adopted in 1999.

African RECs also cannot flourish in the midst of several cross-cutting issues, such as the absence of peace and security, the prevalence of HIV/AIDS, and the accelerating incidence of poverty. Conflict and war do not provide a conducive environment for the successful functioning of RECs. Precious lives and resources are lost and the energies of member states are diverted from the goal of integration. Apart from the dissipation of foreign investment in conflict-prone regions, warring REC countries view each other as enemies and therefore will not work toward a common economic union, regardless of the benefits. Sadly, much of Africa has been saddled with conflict. More than one-half of sub-Saharan African countries have been embroiled in conflict since independence. Indeed, one out of every five Africans currently lives in a country seriously affected by war or strife. The toll of civil strife on the region's economy is very telling. The average civil war in Africa since independence has lasted about seven years and has caused GDP to decline by more than 2 percent for each year of strife. Additionally, it takes on average 14 years after the end of the conflict for a country to recover its level of pre-war growth.[27] The war in the Democratic Republic of the Congo (formerly Zaire) between 1998 and July 2003, which involved as many as eight African nations, no doubt hampered the operations of ECCAS, as Rwanda and Angola (both ECCAS members then) fought on opposing sides. African RECs have began paying attention to peace and security concerns and have put in place formal institutional frameworks to deal with conflict resolution and peacekeeping. ECCAS' Council for Peace and Security in Central Africa as well as SADC's Organ on Politics, Defense, and Security have already been described. COMESA and EAC have also created a Committee on Peace and Security and an Interstate Security Committee respectively. The widely known and by far most advanced REC peacekeeping mechanism in Africa is the Economic Community of West African States Monitoring Group (ECOMOG) created by ECOWAS (see Box 4.3).

HIV/AIDS is another pressing issue for Africa. According to the World Health Organization (WHO), Africa has the greatest burden of HIV/AIDS infections (more on this subject is discussed in Chapter 5). Although it has just over 10 percent of the world's population, by the end of 2006 it accounted for 63 percent of all people living with HIV in the world. In 2006, there were 24.7 million people living with HIV in sub-Saharan Africa, and 2.1 million deaths attributable to the disease. The macroeconomic effects of HIV/AIDS in Africa are substantial, not the least of which is the reduction in labor supply and productivity, through increased mortality and morbidity. This economic impact of HIV/AIDS is also compounded by loss of skills in key sectors of the labor market. The economic impact of the disease on African RECs is aptly reported in an International Labor Organization (ILO) study. According to their estimates, in 2005 six COMESA countries lost 10 percent of their productive workers to the disease, and the labor supply is predicted to contract by same margin, but for a higher number of COMESA countries, eight, by 2010.[28] Even so, it appears that the SADC sub-region has the world's highest levels of HIV prevalence. In Namibia, Lesotho, and South Africa, estimates suggest that more than 20 percent of the population were infected in 2006, while in Botswana and Swaziland nearly 40 percent of the adult populations were affected.[29] African RECs are struggling to come up with a concerted strategy to fight the pandemic, but so far the efforts by SADC appear to be the most far reaching.

The final obstacle for RECs is continent-wide poverty. Africa is home to many of the world's poorest countries. According to the UNDP's 2007 Human Development Index, the bottom 27 out of 175 countries surveyed are in Africa. It is estimated that more than 40 percent of Africa's population lives on less than $1 per day, and nearly 75 percent of all Africans live on less than $2 per day. The region is also the most marginalized in the world. According to the Organization for Economic Cooperation and Development (OECD), Africa's share of global GDP declined by one-third, and its share of world exports fell by two-thirds between 1995 and 2000. Clearly this dire economic scenario poses daunting challenges for the RECs.

African RECs and their key constituents

African RECs will be seen as engines for African development if they are able to surmount the hurdles outlined above. In so doing they will need key actors and partners, with clearly defined roles and mandates in the integration process. We will explore the relationship of African RECs with the AU, the donor community, and the private sector.

For the African RECs to flourish, it will be necessary to establish a robust coordinating mechanism with the continent's supreme organ, the AU, and its proposed AEC. A protocol on the relationship between the AEC and the REC was signed by the OAU (now AU) in February 1998 to provide a framework for closer cooperation, program harmonization and coordination of their activities.[30] In spite of the existence of this protocol, coordination between the AEC and the RECs has been ineffective. For now, the RECs operate almost independently, with very little by way of convergence with the AEC policies and programs. In some cases, the REC integration agenda appears to take precedence over those of the AEC. In any event, the AEC has no framework in place to provide supranational oversight of the activities of the RECs. The problem is compounded because the relationship between the AEC and the AU remain ambiguous at best. The AU ought to take the lead in streamlining the integration agenda. It can begin to do this by becoming the supranational authority required to enforce policy convergence between all the continental integration schemes and also by strengthening the RECs by providing much needed financial and technical support for its operations.

Since nearly all African REC members are recipients of aid and of assistance from the donor community, it is important to examine their attitude and policies regarding regionalism. Though some donors, such as the Club du Sahel,[31] believe that the problems of small countries can "only be solved by regional integration,"[32] the majority of donors, especially the BWIs, do not have integrated programs promoting African RECs. This is because the economic strategy advocated by the BWIs subscribes to trade liberalization, an enhanced role for the private sector, and a less interventionist state. As suggested earlier, the heads of government are the final decision makers in African RECs, so it would seem contradictory for the BWIs to invest economic decision making in the very agent (the state) which it deems wasteful and unproductive. The BWIs maintain instead that the "the private sector should be considered the real beneficiary of regional integration."[33] Not surprisingly, the BWIs draw up country-specific PRSPs, and not regional PRSPs. The BWIs' preference for a state-centric model (rather than an REC model) is based on the assumption that "national actions, and [World] Bank assistance to them, should dominate, except where regional institutions and multicountry efforts would be more effective."[34] Commenting on the lack of donor interest in African RECs, Adebayo Adedeji of the ECA noted that

> the donors are more often than not reluctant to fund regional projects most essential for the success of regional cooperation. Multinational projects are usually of low priority in the investment portfolios of international and regional financial institutions. As for the donors, they do not hide the fact that they prefer bilateral to multinational projects. If multinational projects are to be supported, the funding is usually limited to pre-feasibility and feasibility studies and institution-building.[35]

Notwithstanding this observation, the EU has been a strong champion of African regionalism compared to other donors. This should come as no surprise since the EU is itself a regional institution (see the discussion above on EU and regionalism in Africa).

The final relationship that must be discussed is that between RECs and the private sector. Arguing for a more proactive and visible role for the private sector in the integration process, the ECA writes that "the private sector in most African countries is not part of the identification, formulation, and implementation of integration policies and programs—leaving the burden to government bureaucracies."[36] This observation is very accurate. RECs stand to benefit from private sector involvement either through the provision of human and material resources or through the provision of policy advice and knowledge. And the private sector would undoubtedly gain in scale of operations and efficiency from any mature integration arrangement. At the very least, uniform trade policies across RECs would make it easier for the private sector to invest across countries. However, the private sector's involvement in the integration process has been negligible because of the numerous constraints that African RECs face (outlined above). Of particular note is the precarious investment climate due to issues relating to peace, security and governance, the generally weak macroeconomic environment, and the poor and limited infrastructural resources make the private sector hesitant in advancing the regional integration agenda. Though not widespread, some notable examples of private sector involvement in integration include the Africa Cross Border Initiative: Trade and Investment Facilitation (CBI). The CBI is a framework of harmonized policies to facilitate a market-driven concept of regional integration in Eastern and Southern Africa and Indian Ocean countries, namely Burundi, Comoros, Kenya, Madagascar, Malawi, Mauritius, Namibia, Rwanda, Seychelles, Swaziland, Tanzania, Uganda, Zambia, and Zimbabwe. A marked departure from previous regional initiatives, the Africa Cross Border Initiative specifically proposes the direct involvement of the private sector in the formulation and implementation of African regionalism. In addition, apolitical business networks such as SADC's Chamber of Commerce and the West African Entrepreneurs Network also emphasize the role of the private sector in regionalism. African RECs can empower the private sector by granting specific provisions in treaties and protocols that alleviate the concerns of the private sector.

Conclusions: the future of regionalism in Africa

RECs are an increasingly important feature of the global trade architecture. Indeed, the sharp increase in the number of RECs worldwide since the millennium has led some to conclude that a third wave of regional integration is currently underway.[37] Despite the limited success of African RECs, they will continue to be an important institutional framework for Africa's development. Potential benefits such as economies of scale as well as enhanced bargaining positions are all powerful incentives for Africa to continue to push the REC mechanism. As mentioned earlier, support from economic arrangements with external actors, such as the EU under the Cotonou agreement, are indicators that the allure of regionalism in Africa will persist in the foreseeable future. To realize the ultimate goal of creating the AEC, a necessary and desirable institution for the continent, the pace of regionalism must be hastened through serious political commitment from Africa's leaders. Green and Seidman made an astute observation on the indispensability of a continental African economic bloc. They noted that:

> Africa as a whole could provide markets able to support large-scale efficient industrial complexes; no single African state nor existing sub-regional economic union can do so. African states cannot establish large-scale productive complexes stimulating demand throughout the economy as poles of rapid economic growth because their markets are far too small. Instead the separate tiny economies willy-nilly plan on lines leading to the dead ends of excessive dependence on raw material exports and small scale inefficient "national factories" at high costs per unit of output. Inevitably, therefore, they fail to reduce substantially their basic dependence on foreign markets, complex manufactures and capital.[38]

It has been 40 years since Green and Seidman offered these insights yet nothing fundamental has changed about the structure of African economies. This is because African leaders have so far only paid lip service to the idea of political unity. Indeed, one can argue that the economic situation in Africa has not been promising because of the lack of political cohesion. Ghana's Kwame Nkrumah warned similarly that, short of the creation of an African common market, African RECs would become an impediment in Africa's march to true development. And he argued further that such a common market would not materialize if Africa were not united politically. He said: "the lack of political unity places inter African economic institutions at the mercy of powerful, foreign commercial interests, and sooner or later these will use such institutions as funnels through which to pour money for the continued exploitation of Africa."[39] The problem of the transformation of African economies must thus be pursued in tandem with serious continental political arrangements.

5 Emerging issues and future direction

Tangible and sustainable development continues to elude Africa despite the concerted efforts of national governments, external actors, and other interested publics. Most objective human development indicators show Africa as the region that has made the least progress amongst developing countries. The proportion of those suffering from malnutrition and hunger has increased, life expectancies have fallen due to HIV/AIDS, and the burdens of debt and poverty are accelerating across the region. According to the World Bank, growth per head between 1960 and 2000 in sub-Saharan Africa averaged 0.8 percent per year, compared with an average of 2.3 percent for all of the world's developing countries.[1] Though Africa's recent growth performance has been encouraging, with real GDP (gross domestic product) growth averaging 5 percent for the fifth consecutive year, these developments are uneven and fragile. In the short term, global economic emergencies in the food and energy markets and the prospect of stagflation in mature industrial economies make these gains tentative at best. In the long term, however, this encouraging aggregate macroeconomic output does not seem sustainable, as it rests on very weak structural foundations and a high and heavy debt overhang. The underlying human capital formation and the structure of sub-Saharan Africa's economies has not changed much since independence. The export of raw materials and minerals continues to be the mainstay of most of the African economies, making them susceptible to shock and systemic risks. Furthermore, Africa's economies are debt-ridden. In 2005, sub-Saharan Africa's external debt amounted to $239.4 billion, compared to $3 billion in 1960. The vulnerability of Africa's economies, despite recent growth, is aptly captured by the ECA in its *2008 Economic Report on Africa*. It states that, "Africa's overall economic performance has improved since adoption of the Monterrey Consensus in 2002. However, this has not translated adequately into progress with poverty reduction, the ultimate objective. Africa, particularly Africa excluding North Africa, is still the region with the highest percentage of people living in extreme poverty and deprivation."[2] This chapter will explore these and other trends in African development today and detail the responses by the African IEOs to tackle these challenges.

Africa and the MDGs

The ECA, ADB and NEPAD have all endorsed the MDGs. Indeed, the founding document of NEPAD pledges to ensure that the continent achieves these goals and targets (see Chapter 1). So, with the world, and Africa, halfway to the 2015 target date on achieving the MDGs, it is worth reviewing the progress made thus far and the role played by African IEOs in meeting the MDGs' 8 goals and 21 targets (see Box 5.1 for the stated goals). The prognosis, thus far, for meeting the MDGs in Africa has not been good. The region is way off track in meeting the targets. In 2007, the ADB reported that only three countries, Botswana, Cape Verde, and Ghana were "on track" to reach at least five of the eight goals. It is estimated that at current rates, the targets for halving poverty will not be met in Africa until 2150 (some 135 years late); the target of achieving universal primary education will not be met until 2130 (115 years late); and that for reducing child deaths by 2165 (150 years after the MDG deadline).[3] The lack of progress by Africa on the MDGs prompted the launch of the MDG Africa Steering Group on 14 September 2007. The group, chaired by the UN secretary-general, brings together the heads of the ADB, AU Commission, European Commission, IMF, Islamic Development Bank, and the World Bank to identify the practical steps needed to help Africa realize the MDGs on time.[4]

The UN (in partnership with Cisco and Google) has since, on 1 November 2007, launched a website, the *MDG Monitor*, to shows how countries are progressing in their efforts to achieve the MDGs. Users can access MDG-related information about 130 countries worldwide. A special feature of the site is Google Earth, which allows users to view country profiles in three dimensions.

The ECA has responded to the MDG challenge mainly through knowledge generation and management. In 2005, the ECA, with support from the United Nations Department of Economic and Social Affairs (DESA), launched the Knowledge Sharing Project (KSP) on Poverty Reduction Strategies and Millennium Development Goals. The KSP is a product of a series of meetings of the African Learning Group on Poverty Reduction Strategy Papers (PRSP-LG), established

Box 5.1 The Millennium Development Goals (MDGs)

At the UN's Millennium Assembly in September 2000, the UN agreed to a set of eight MDGs for the world's poor nations to be achieved by 2015. The goals are:

1 Eradicate extreme poverty and hunger

- Reduce by half the proportion of people living on less than a dollar a day.
- Achieve full and productive employment and decent work for all, including women and young people.
- Reduce by half the proportion of people who suffer from hunger.

2 Achieve universal primary education

- Ensure that all boys and girls complete a full course of primary schooling.

3 Promote gender equality and empower women

- Eliminate gender disparity in primary and secondary education preferably by 2005, and at all levels by 2015.

4 Reduce child mortality

- Reduce by two-thirds the mortality rate among children under five.

5 Improve maternal health

- Reduce by three-quarters the maternal mortality ratio.
- Achieve, by 2015, universal access to reproductive health.

6 Combat HIV/AIDS, malaria, and other diseases

- Halt and begin to reverse the spread of HIV/AIDS.
- Achieve, by 2010, universal access to treatment for HIV/AIDS for all those who need it.
- Halt and begin to reverse the incidence of malaria and other major diseases.

(*Box continued on next page*)

7 Ensure environmental sustainability

- Integrate the principles of sustainable development into country policies and programs; reverse loss of environmental resources.
- Reduce biodiversity loss, achieving, by 2010, a significant reduction in the rate of loss.
- Reduce by half the proportion of people without sustainable access to safe drinking water and basic sanitation.
- Achieve significant improvement in lives of at least 100 million slum dwellers, by 2020.

8 Develop a global partnership for development

- Develop further an open trading and financial system that is rule-based, predictable and non-discriminatory, includes a commitment to good governance, development and poverty reduction — nationally and internationally.
- Address the least developed countries' special needs. This includes tariff- and quota-free access for their exports; enhanced debt relief for heavily indebted poor countries; cancellation of official bilateral debt; and more generous official development assistance for countries committed to poverty reduction.
- Address the special needs of landlocked and small island developing states.
- Deal comprehensively with developing countries' debt problems through national and international measures to make debt sustainable in the long term.
- In cooperation with the developing countries, develop decent and productive work for youth.
- In cooperation with pharmaceutical companies, provide access to affordable essential drugs in developing countries.
- In cooperation with the private sector, make available the benefits of new technologies — especially information and communications technologies.

Source: www.un.org/millenniumgoals (General Assembly resolution 55/2, 19–20, UN Doc. A/RES/55/2-Sept. 18, 2000). The *MDG Monitor*, www.mdgmonitor.org

Note: For useful critiques of the MDGs, see Samir Amin, "The Millennium Development Goals: A Critique from the South," *Monthly Review* (March 2006): 1–5; and William Easterly, *How the MDGs Are Unfair to Africa*, Brookings Institution, Working Paper no. 14 (Washington, DC: Brookings Institution Press, 2007).

in 1999 to provide a forum for the exchange of views and articulation of an African position on the Poverty Reduction Strategy Papers (PRSPs). The KSP is managed by the MDG's Poverty Analysis and Monitoring Section in the African Centre for Gender and Social Development. The ECA has also introduced the MDG Mapper, a web toll that allows for the dynamic mapping of comparative progress by African countries toward achieving the MDGs. For countries making the least progress, the Mapper enables the calculation of the extent to which they are off target (see www.geoinfo.uneca.org/mdg). The ECA's MDG efforts are further reflected in initiatives such as the ECA's Annual MDG Report to the AU Summit.

The ADB too is engaged on the MDG goals on several fronts. As mentioned earlier, the head of the ADB is part of the UN secretary-general's Africa MDG Steering Group. In addition to its regular operations and financial assistance to regional member countries the Bank has embarked on new initiatives. The first is the Bank's Water Supply and Sanitation Initiative (RWSSI). This has the objective of accelerating access to a sustainable safe water supply and basic sanitation in rural Africa, aiming to reach coverage of 80 percent by 2015. Second, the Bank has moved to help post-conflict countries clear their arrears with the Bank by establishing the Post-Conflict Countries Facility (PCCF). So far, two countries—Burundi and Congo—have benefited from the Facility. The Bank is also involved in debt relief initiatives, described later in this section.

The outcome of MDGs is also closely aligned with the future of NEPAD (see Chapter 1). According to Professor Wiseman Nkuhlu, the past CEO of the NEPAD Secretariat,

> NEPAD will be judged by progress towards the MDGs. In Africa, the achievement of the MDGs means social and economic development on an unprecedented scale. NEPAD is committed to joining forces with business, civil society and our development partners to ensure this occurs and that each of us honors our commitments under the New Partnership for Africa's Development. Bending the Arc provides a forum for engaging all stakeholders to mobilize resources to obtain the MDGs in Africa in partnership with the G-8.[5]

These sentiments were echoed by Kofi Annan when he noted to the UN General Assembly on 16 September 2002 that, "there is a symbiotic relationship between NEPAD and the Millennium Development Goals ... The NEPAD will not be a success if Africa fails to achieve the goals—and the world as a whole cannot achieve the goals unless they are achieved in Africa."[6]

Particularly important for the MDGs are efforts aimed at combating AIDS, malaria, and other diseases. In this regards the task remains Herculean, with merely four African countries on track to meet the MDG targets. With more than 20 million African deaths from the disease alone, and the number of new tuberculosis cases increasing (tuberculosis increased from 148 per 100,000 in 1990 to 281 per 100,000 in 2004), HIV/AIDS poses the greatest development challenge for Africa in recent times. African IEOs, specifically the ECA and ADB, have put in place strategies and modalities to deal with the pandemic. In February 2003, the ECA launched the Commission on HIV/AIDS and Governance in Africa (CHGA). It was convened by the UN secretary-general, Kofi Annan and chaired by the ECA's executive secretary K.Y. Amoako in response to the threat to Africa's governance and development posed by the HIV/AIDS epidemic. Over its two-year lifetime, CHGA's research objectives were threefold: first, to help African policymakers to understand the nature of the long-term development challenges posed by HIV/AIDS; second, to assist African policymakers in devising appropriate policies and programs to help treat Africans already living with HIV/AIDS; and finally, to assist policymakers in understanding both the fiscal and structural implications of HIV-related medication in resource-limited settings. CHGA's work was guided by 20 high-profile commissioners, including Joy Phumaphi, assistant director-general of the World Health Organization, Peter Piot, head of UNAIDS, South African researcher Alan Whiteside, and Richard Feachem, executive director of the Global Fund to Fight AIDS, Tuberculosis and Malaria. The former Zambian president Kenneth Kaunda and former prime minister of Mozambique Pascoal Mocumbi served as CHGA's patrons. A final report on CHGAs work, "Securing Our Future," was presented to UN secretary-general Ban Ki-moon in June 2008. The report cited many specific cultural factors in Africa, including gender inequalities, wife inheritance and some sexual practices, which fuel the spread of AIDS and undermine the effectiveness of national responses to the epidemic. Prior to the formation of CHGA, the ECA consistently raised HIV/AIDS in development forums and engaged in partnerships with other organizations to raise awareness of the pandemic. The ECA's African Development Forum's 2000 conference was themed "AIDS: Africa's Greatest Leadership Challenge."

The ADB tackles the HIV/AIDS issue by providing assistance to its members in two ways: it helps member states to develop and implement multi-sectoral HIV/AIDS prevention and control activities; and it supports programs prepared and led by specialized UN agencies and other development partners in the fight against HIV/AIDS, such as the Joint United Nations Program on HIV/AIDS (UNAIDS). The Bank aims to mainstream HIV/AIDS programs in all its operations. For example, the Bank provides analysis of HIV/AIDS in the PRSPs and Bank Country Strategy Papers for its regional members and screens their project and program proposals to ensure that HIV/AIDS dimensions are fully taken into account and reflected in project design. The Bank thus sees the spread of HIV/AIDS as a multi-sector challenge and has called for increased coordination in infrastructure programs. For example, transport routes and construction sites are documented sectors where there is a high incidence of HIV infection. Toward this end, the Bank, in August 2006, signed the "Joint Initiative by Development Agencies for the Infrastructure Sectors to Mitigate the Spread of HIV/AIDS" with six other development partners.[7] Currently the Bank is funding about 60 health interventions throughout the continent for a total sum of $US835 million, with HIV/AIDS representing approximately 15 percent (or $125 million) of that investment. Beyond support for member countries the Bank supports HIV/AIDS initiatives through RECs, such as SADC's support of the HIV/AIDS, Malaria and TB project that, among other things, addresses the clinical needs of AIDS orphans. Other regional supports are provided by way of investments made through three projects, namely the Lake Chad Basin project, the Mano-River HIV/AIDS control project, and the Sexually Transmitted Infections/HIV/AIDS Initiative of Riverain States along the Congo, Ubangi and Shari Rivers.[8]

Though it is the latest African IEO, NEPAD curiously does not present HIV/AIDS as a priority area of development (see the critique by African civil society groups, "NEPAD and Human Rights," in Appendix 1). It must be quickly added that there exist, to name a few, several prominent continent-wide HIV/AIDS initiatives such as the International Partnership against AIDS in Africa and the AIDS Watch Africa Group of Heads of State formed at the AU's 2001 Abuja summit on AIDS, Malaria, and Other Infectious Diseases.

Debt and corruption

Debt continues to be one issue that has put a severe drain on Africa's economic development. In 2005, sub-Saharan Africa's level of official (non-concessional) external debt amounted to $239 billion, compared to $3 billion in 1960. To help ensure that the world's poorest countries reduce their debts to "sustainable levels," the World Bank and IMF, in 1996, launched an initiative for heavily indebted poor countries (HIPCs). Of the 38 eligible countries, 32 are from sub-Saharan Africa. The HIPC guidelines require a candidate country to complete a three-year IMF and World Bank supported adjustment and reform program. These reforms include economic stabilization programs, restructuring state-owned enterprises, targeting public spending toward poverty reduction, and health and education programs. To date, debt reduction packages have been approved for 33 countries, 27 of them in Africa, providing US$49 billion (net present value terms as of the decision point) in debt-service relief over time. In 2005, to help accelerate progress toward the MDGs, the HIPC Initiative was supplemented by the Multilateral Debt Relief Initiative (MDRI). The MDRI allows for 100 percent relief on eligible debts by three multilateral institutions, the IMF, the International Development Association (IDA) of the World Bank, and the ADB for countries completing the HIPC initiative process. The MDRI initiative came about because the G-8 came to the conclusion that excessive debt burden of the very poor countries was not only unsustainable but that the debt negatively impacted their ability to make progress on the development front. These countries were able to service their debt obligations only because the multilaterals offered them new grants and loans to help them repay their old ones. This recycling of funds, while making the balance sheets of the World Bank and the IMF look better than they really were, had no practical impact on the overall development of the countries. So under the MDRI, the World Bank, IMF, and ADB will stop collecting debts and cut the flow of new money to these countries by the same amount. So far, 33 African countries have benefited from $8.5 billion in debt relief under the MDRI.

While these two initiatives have provided much-needed borrowing space to many African countries, it is essential that the money be put to productive use and to avoid the risk of a new debt overhang problem emerging. NEPAD has been criticized for not going far enough in its proposals with regards to debt cancellation and for failing to delink debt relief from the continuation of neoliberal structural adjustment policies. The ECA meanwhile has called for the expansion of HIPC and MDRI initiatives. According to the ECA,

> Although significant progress has been made on debt relief in the last two years, there is need to extend eligibility for current debt relief programs to non-HIPC African countries. It is also important to reduce the number of years it takes for countries to move from

decision to completion points in the HIPC program. African countries should also put in place a mechanism to ensure that loans from new creditors do not lead to a new cycle of indebtedness.[9]

The ECA call for expansion of these two initiatives is especially important since new creditors, such as China and India, normally offer concessional loans for African countries with more flexible disbursement criteria than the traditional Paris Club creditors.

Beyond managing Africa's excessive debt, access to finance or new monies is critical to Africa's overall economic development. In 2004 for instance Jeffery Sachs and others estimated that sub-Saharan Africa would need about $25 billion in additional assistance per year in order to meet the MDG targets.[10] The challenge then is to mobilize significant domestic and international financial resources. In 2007, the ECA surveyed African policymakers to find out what factors hindered the mobilization of domestic resources. The greatest obstacle in the study was weak financial infrastructure (30.8 percent), followed by governance issues (26.9 percent), and corruption (12.8 percent).[11] Whether African governments will be able to translate the results of the ECA study into tangible policy action remains to be seen.

Corruption

No discussion on Africa's future development would be complete without addressing the issue of corruption. As John Githongo, a former anti-corruption czar in Kenya, rightly noted, corruption "is at the epicentre of the failure by many African countries to achieve economic objectives so finely articulated in their development plans."[12] Though corruption is a global phenomenon, Africa appears as to be the most corrupt region in the world.[13] The endemic nature of the corruption in Africa is captured in an AU report which estimates that Africa loses $148 billion, or a quarter of its entire GDP to corruption *every year.*[14]

Not surprisingly, all African IEOs have anti-corruption mechanisms in place. The ECA in 2006 and 2007, for example, conducted a study on: "Deepening Judiciary Effectiveness in Combating Corruption" and convened two ad hoc expert meetings on the findings of that study. The ECA hopes to publish its findings soon. The ECA is also currently undertaking a study to assess the efficiency and impact of national anti-corruption institutions in Africa. In addition, the ECA plans to launch an online anti-corruption web portal in the near future. The ECA believes that the only way corruption can be stamped out in Africa is if all major stakeholders, including the judiciary, national anti-corruption institutions, parliament and the pan-African body of national anti-corruption institutions in Africa, work hand-in-hand. According to Okey Onyejekwe, director of ECA's GPAD, "the fight against corruption cannot simply be limited to the state, there must also be political commitment. Until it becomes a battle that engages all stakeholders, stand-alone interventions such as the establishment of national corruption commissions ... won't make a difference."[15]

The ADB's policy on Good Governance (approved by its board of directors in 1999) and its guidelines approved in 2001 identify combating corruption as one of the five key prerequisites for good governance in Africa. According to the ADB, "corruption weakens core democratic values, challenges political stability, undermines the credibility of public institutions, and erodes the consolidation of good governance."[16] The Bank's recent initiatives aimed at curbing corruption include the Anti-money Laundering and Asset Recovery strategy. Launched in October 2007, the anti-money laundering strategy seeks to strengthen internal safeguards against money laundering (in particular, financial sector operations) and to support the efforts of its regional members in combating corruption and money laundering, especially at the regional level. On 16 December 2008, the ABD partnered with the OECD to support the efforts of African governments and business to fight corruption and bribery and to boost corporate accountability.

Like the other African IEOs, NEPAD identifies corruption as one of the chief obstacles to the continent's development. NEPAD has an "action plan" in place "to combat and eradicate corruption"[17] on the continent.[18] A close reading of NEPAD's declarations on corruption shows that they are aspirational goals and not action plans. The NEPAD "action plan" wants "to ensure the effective functioning of parliaments and other accountability institutions in our respective countries, including parliamentary committees and anti-corruption bodies; and to ensure the independence of the judicial system that will be able to prevent abuse of power and corruption,"[19] but it tells us nothing about what specific mechanisms will be put in place to prevent graft. To be sure, NEPAD has the voluntary peer review mechanism on good governance (see Box 2.1) but it will remain weak since it has no enforcement capacity.

Part of the problem with the African IEOs' anti-corruption initiatives is that ultimate compliance with them rests with the African heads of states who themselves in most cases are the beneficiaries of graft. Perhaps one way to resolve this dilemma is to heed the advice of Wafula and Okumu in their call for a new anti-corruption architecture that is bottom-up, rather than top-down. Such a strategy, they write, "would entail strengthening national legislation, tightening procedures and audit systems, improving public service performance, developing a culture of outrage, positively encouraging public service integrity, and strengthening governance structures."[20]

China, India, and Africa

China and India, over the last decade or so, have established themselves as increasingly influential and strategic actors across Africa. How exactly have the African IEOs reacted to the increasing presence of China and India in Africa, and what strategies do they have in place to make the encounters with these emerging powers beneficial to the continent? Contemporary China–Africa diplomatic relations are over half a century old, but China's rapid economic growth has fueled demand for raw materials and energy and hence its keen engagement with Africa. China is now Africa's third most important trading partner, behind the USA and France, with trade volume in 2006 totaling $55.5 billion, compared to just $4 billion a decade ago (1996). The value of China's trade with Africa is predicted to reach the $100 billion mark in the next five years. In its dealings with Africa, China pledges to adhere to its five principles of peaceful coexistence, which emphasize: non-interference and respect for African countries' independent choice of development path, mutual benefit and reciprocity, non-aggression, interaction based on equality, and consultation and cooperation in global affairs. The China/Africa trade, investment, and economic relationship is being consolidated by Chinese initiatives such as the Asia–Africa Summit, the China–Africa Cooperation Forum (FOCAC), and the China–Africa Business Council.

Chinese economic forays on the continent are particularly felt at the ADB. China, a non-regional member of the ADB since 1985, currently, has 24,230 shares, or a 1.117 percent stake in the Bank. Since joining, China has donated $314 million to the African Development Fund, and has supported numerous infrastructure construction, poverty alleviation, and education projects in the continent. China and the ADB signed a $2 million technical cooperation agreement in 1996, and China hosted ADB's annual board meeting in 2007, the first time that the annual board meeting of the ADB was held in Asia and the second time outside Africa. In 2001, the meetings took place in Spain.

Not to be outdone, India too is also consolidating its growing presence in Africa. Driven by the same strategic needs as China, India has seen a massive upturn in its trade relations with the continent. Trade between the two sides has increased tenfold since the last decade. Trade in 2005 rose to $9 billion compared to $967 million in 1990. Over the past five years India has offered lines of concessionary credit to Africa worth $2.5 billion, and it plans on a $10 billion investment fund for the continent. To cement its diplomatic profile in Africa, India in April 2008 hosted the inaugural India–Africa Forum in Delhi, with fourteen African heads of government in attendance. Like China, India is a non-regional member of the ADB, having joined the Bank in 1983. It has sponsored development projects in conjunction with ABD and NEPAD. In July 2002, India hosted a conference on NEPAD themed "India and NEPAD: Furthering India and Africa Economic Cooperation," and in 2004, India proposed to create a $200 million line of credit for NEPAD projects.

China and India's deeper engagement with Africa offers both opportunity and cause for caution. NEPAD is being positioned as a platform that can best manage these ties. NEPAD's CEO, Firmino Mucavele, notes that in these new relationships NEPAD can "see in India and China an opportunity to convert our comparative advantage into competitiveness,"[21] though he admits Africa lacks a clear and coordinated strategy on how to engage these emerging powers constructively.

The African Union

Much of the success of Africa's economic institutions depends on the power accorded it by the AU. The AU is after all the supreme political organ of the continent, and from which most of the African IEOs gather their mandate. Indeed, in March 2007, the AU decided that NEPAD should be integrated into the structures and processes of the AU by July 2008.[22]

Interestingly, the AU has committed itself to new economic institutions of its own. The AU charter names three bodies: the African Central Bank, the African Monetary Fund, and the African Investment Bank. Of these, only the African Investment Bank (to be based in Tripoli, Libya) has been established, though it is not yet functional. The mandate of the African Investment Bank is to foster economic growth and the acceleration of economic integration in Africa. The specific tasks charged to the African Investment Bank are: to promote investment activities of the public and private sector intended to advance regional integration of the member states of the AU; to utilize available resources for the implementation of investment projects contributing to the strengthening of the private sector and the modernization of rural sector activities in low-income African countries; to mobilize resources from capital markets inside and outside Africa for the financing of investment projects in African countries; to provide technical assistance as may be needed in African countries for the study, preparation, financing, and execution of investment projects; and to undertake other activities and services that may contribute to the fulfillment of its overall mandate.

Given the operational difficulties facing the ADB it seems rather odd that the AU is bent on creating more financial institutions. Of course, there is nothing wrong conceptually with new African IEOs. The issue here is that some of the proposed entities (in particular the African Investment Bank) appear to have mandates which duplicate those of the ADB. Given the extremely limited resources of the AU, it is imperative that it defines and clarifies the roles of the key players in Africa's integration process in order to avoid wasteful overlap of its institutional arrangements.

With respect to the ECA, it appears that the introduction of NEPAD shifted the momentum for policymaking from the UN body to the AU. It has been noted elsewhere that ECA contributed to the formation of NEPAD. However, the impetus and drive for the NEPAD came not from the ECA but from a handful of AU leaders.[23] The decision to incorporate NEPAD within the structures of the AU has in some ways further isolated the ECA's role as the originator of African development policy. As Eddy Maloka sees it, "The non-involvement of the ECA in the early phases of the NEPAD process may have affected the extent to which the NEPAD base document could dialogue with previous initiatives, of course, but perhaps this is also a signal for the beginning of a new power relationship between the ECA and the continent's states,"[24] a shift which he views positively.

Conclusion

The development challenges facing Africa are enormous and African IEOs, given their mandate, have an important role to play. It seems, however, that African IEOs and African leaders have not been effective in ensuring sustainable development because rather than taking the lead role in the search for answers to Africa's economic problems, they have assigned their economic fate to global IEOs that prescribe one-size-fits-all economic models (see Chapter 3). African IEOs need to reclaim policy autonomy and space in the design and implementation of economic policy. Africa leaders for their part need to take pan-African unity seriously and work toward political unification. At the launch of the OAU in 1963, Kwame Nkrumah reminded his counterpart African presidents of the necessity of harmonizing policies and uniting Africa. He said: "Here is a challenge which destiny has thrown out to the leaders of Africa. It is for us to grasp that golden opportunity to prove that the genius of African people can surmount the separatist tendencies in sovereign nationhood by coming together speedily, for the sake of Africa's greater glory and infinite well being, into a Union of African States."[25] It has been some 46 years since Nkrumah sounded the clarion call. African IEOs and African leaders, for the betterment of their peoples, ought to respond.

Appendix 1
African Civil Society Declaration on NEPAD

"We do not accept NEPAD!!"

"Africa is not for sale!!"

We members of social movements, trade unions, youth and women's organizations, faith-based organizations, academics, NGOs, and other popular civil society organizations from the whole of Africa, meeting in Port Shepstone, South Africa, 4–8 July 2002, on the threshold of the launch of the African Union and the New Partnership for Africa's Development (NEPAD) in Durban, critically examined NEPAD in the context of the struggles for Africa's development and emancipation.

While conscious of the importance of joint endeavors for the development of Africa, this "new international partnership" initiative ignores and sidelines past and existing programs and efforts by Africans themselves to resolve Africa's crises and move forward from programs such as the Lagos Plan of Action (1980) and the Abuja Treaty (1991), the African Alternative Framework to Structural Adjustment Program (AAF-SAAP, 1989), the African Charter for Popular Participation and Development (Arusha Charter, 1990) and the Cairo Agenda (1994).

In contrast to such programs, NEPAD is mainly concerned with raising external financial resources, appealing to and relying on external governments and institutions. In addition, it is a top-down program driven by African elites and drawn up with the corporate forces and institutional instruments of globalization, rather than being based on African people's experiences, knowledge, and demands. A legitimate African program has to start from the people and be owned by the people.

We take as our point of departure, and build upon, the many fundamental critiques of NEPAD from all over the continent, such as the statements of the African Social Forum (Bamako, Mali, January 2002) and of CODESRIA (Council for Development and Social Science

Research in Africa) with the Third World Network–Africa (Accra, April 2002) and others.

During our deliberations and wide-ranging discussions on NEPAD we focused on the following key aspects and reached the following conclusions.

I NEPAD, democracy, and good governance

We discussed the nature and role of the post-colonial state in Africa, and the role of the developmental state in the earlier economic, social, and human development achievements following independence. We noted that NEPAD

- ignores the way the state has, itself, been undermined as a social provider and vehicle for development, particularly under the World Bank's tutelage;
- ignores the way that the structurally adjusted state has, in turn, been undermining institutions and processes of democracy in Africa;
- does not reflect the historic struggles in Africa for participatory forms of democracy and decentralization of power;
- promises of democracy and good governance, are largely intended to satisfy foreign donors and to give guarantees to foreign investment.

We conclude that

1 While we are committed to good government in Africa, we do not accept the interpretation and content that this is given in NEPAD, including questionable economic policies that we do not accept embedded within good governance,
2 We call on African people to mobilize for a developmental participatory state responsive to their needs and aspirations, and to build popular and democratic movements that can hold our states to their responsibilities.

II NEPAD, peace, and stability

We discussed how the conflicts on the continent have their sources in the legacy of colonialism, economic exclusion, political intolerance, social polarization, artificial borders and unequal access to resources. We noted that NEPAD

- ignores all these factors and approaches these problems mainly as technical peace-keeping operations;

- does not point to the structural adjustment policies of the IMF and World Bank in exacerbating conflicts leading to further wars;
- does not point to the interests of corporations, war profiteers and war-lords, in their determination to control and exploit our resources, such as oil, diamonds, and other precious resources, as a major source of war and conflict in Africa.

We conclude that

1 Peace based on and guaranteeing human security requires an environment that fulfils people's needs, and livelihood needs free from all forms of discrimination.
2 Peace demands a Pan-African response to the divisions and tensions created by the legacy of arbitrary colonial borders and divisive social relations.
3 The Kampala Declaration establishing the Conference on Security, Stability, Development and Cooperation (CSSDCA) can be an important instrument for peace building.

III NEPAD and human rights

We discussed with great concern the longstanding denial and abuse of human rights in most of the countries of Africa and the devastating effects of the HIV-AIDS pandemic on our people. We noted that NEPAD

- makes very few references to human rights and these are largely rhetorical;
- deals only superficially with the impact of HIV-AIDS upon people's lives;
- does not guarantee self-determination for the people and contains policies that contradict or are incompatible with democracy and human rights;
- promotes regional economic integration but is totally silent on the rights of people to freely move and seek employment across borders in Africa.

We noted, further, that since the recent G8 meeting in Kananaskis, NEPAD is now being linked to the US agenda on terrorism, that could be used as a lever for the introduction of legislation violating basic civil and political rights.

We commit ourselves to continue our struggle for human rights in the fullest meaning, including political, civil, economic, social, women's, cultural, and environmental rights.

IV NEPAD and structural adjustment programmes

We analyzed the policies and effects, and our direct experiences of World Bank SAPs over recent decades in our countries. We noted that, despite the negative economic, social, political, and environmental effects of SAPs, NEPAD

- accepts the fundamentals of the neo-liberal and gender-blind SAPs paradigm which has been largely responsible for the deepening of the African crises, including the feminization of poverty;
- uncritically endorses the latest version of SAPs, the so-called Poverty Reduction Strategy Program (PRSPs) which have been discredited by popular movements;
- throws a lifeline to the IMF and WB at precisely the time that they are in ideological and institutional crises as a result of unremitting criticism and struggles worldwide against their policies.

We commit ourselves

- To continue to expose to greater public knowledge, and reinforce our resistance to all policies of the IMF and the World Bank now incorporated into NEPAD.

V NEPAD and resource mobilization

We examined the challenges and problems of resource mobilization for development, and noted that NEPAD

- ignores the question of people's ownership and control of African resources, and disregards the people as the most vital resource and purpose of development;
- will not mobilize Africa's rich natural resources for African development but for further foreign exploitation and plunder;
- has nothing to say about the mobilization, redistribution and utilization of African land for development, particularly for women;
- focuses heavily on external financial resources without concern for the costs, and the negative economic, social, and environmental effects of foreign investment and liberalized capital flows.

We conclude that:

1 The unrealistic hopes for external financial resources will, as always, not be forthcoming, as already evident in the recent G8 response to NEPAD.
2 The donors, or aid givers have shown that they will decide separately which countries they will/will not support and on their own policy terms and self-interests.
3 The debt relief offers by the G8 will, similarly, be very limited and only offered to those governments which dutifully follow neo-liberal and gender-blind precepts.
4 Such limited debt relief, will, nonetheless, not go even to such countries but to bail out the creditors.
5 The whole NEPAD fundraising project is a non-starter, and we will focus our efforts on appropriate resource mobilization, including African financial resources now legally and illegally outside of Africa; and relate all such resources to alternative development strategies based on collective self-reliance.

VI NEPAD and debt

We examined the nature, sources, and causes of Africa's debt, which is a fundamental cause of underdevelopment, poverty, and inequality; is owed to the same forces that benefited from slavery, colonialism, and neo-colonialism; has served to build the wealth and power of the elites in Africa; and is not only a financial, but a political instrument of domination and control of the North over Africa.

We note, however, that NEPAD

- accepts the obligation for Africa to repay this illegitimate debt to the further prejudice of fundamentally important social services and development needs;
- ignores the demands for total debt cancellation produced by campaigns in Africa, in South–South campaigns and worldwide.

On this basis we

1 We demand total and unconditional debt cancellation.
2 We reaffirm the demand for reparations for the social, economic, and ecological damage done to Africa and its people through slavery and colonialism.
3 We call for the return of Africa's wealth corruptly transferred by African elites and held in the North.

4   We undertake to intensify popular mobilization to pressurize African governments to repudiate the debt.

VII NEPAD, trade, and globalization

We fully discussed the role of trade in Africa and the current global system, and noted that indiscriminate trade liberalization has led to de-industrialization, increased unemployment and growing poverty, and has reinforced Africa's role in the global economy as suppliers of cheap raw materials and labor.

We noted that NEPAD

- ignores experience and the huge body of evidence and analyses discrediting the theories that trade leads to growth which leads to development;
- accepts export-led growth and the expansion of Africa's traditional exports which has already aggravated the deteriorating terms of trade for Africa;
- reinforces Africa's focus on market access into the richest countries through unilateral but false offers such as the EU's Everything But Arms (EBA);
- endorses the aims of reciprocal free trade and other policy conditionalities demanded by the EU and the US, such as privatization, labor deregulation, and investment liberalization in the Cotonou Agreement and the African Growth and Opportunities Act (AGOA), respectively;
- accepts the erroneous depiction of the "marginalization" of Africa, whereas Africa has long been deeply and disadvantageously integrated into the global economy;
- promotes the deeper integration of Africa into the current globalization process which fundamentally serves the interests of the rich;
- misunderstands the imbalanced nature of WTO trade agreements and trade-related agreements, particularly the General Agreement on Trade in Services which will extend global appropriation of African services and resources.

We conclude that

1   We need to continue our efforts to create different types of local, regional and inter-regional trade, and a different role for trade in our economies.

2 We will continue to campaign for our governments to resist unilateral, bilateral and multilateral trade agreements which do not
address the inequities of the international economic system.

3 We will continue to campaign and mobilize the African peoples to
pressurize their governments to resist an expansion of the scope and
powers of the WTO through the introduction of ever more new
issues, and to resist a new WTO round being pushed since the Doha
Ministerial Conference.

4 We will continue to build the popular movement at national, continental and international levels against neo-liberal economic globalization, and against the World Trade Organization as the main
institutional force driving globalization.

On the basis of the above, we do not accept the NEPAD plan, as a
process and in its content. We are to committed to joint efforts for
Africa's development and emancipation, and we call upon all African
peoples' organizations and movements to continue their longstanding
efforts to produce sustainable, just and viable alternatives that will
benefit all the people of Africa.

"Another Africa is possible !"

"Another world is possible !!"

Source: www.ifg.org/wssd/acsnepad_decl.htm

Appendix 2

Summary of African Development Bank Group activities

Table A2.1 Loans made by the ADB (US$, million)

	2004		2005		Cumulative total*	
ADB loans						
Number	23		34		991	
Amount approved	2,359	0.86	1,241	0.65	31,519	0.18
Disbursements	978	0.76	850	0.92	20,185	0.84
ADF loans and grants						
Number	99		65		2,045	
Amount approved	1,953	0.55	2,032	0.02	23,236	0.52
Disbursements	1,056	0.82	987	0.72	12,892	0.32
NTF loans						
Number	2		3		75	
Amount approved	14	0.37	4	0.56	406	0.76
Disbursements	7	0.47	4	0.85	260	0.05
Group total						
Number	124		102		3,111	
Amount approved	4,327	0.78	3,278	0.23	55,162	0.45
Disbursements	2,043	0.05	1,843	0.48	33,338	0.21

Source: *Annual Report* 2005, www.afdb.org

Note:
*Since the initial operations of the three institutions (1967 for ADB, 1974 for ADF and 1976 for NTF).

Table A2.2 Group loan and grant approvals by country (millions of UA)

Country	2004		2005		Cumulative total*	
Algeria	–		–		1,889	0.1
Angola	–		17	0.5	339	0.4
Benin	21	0.2	59	0.5	489	0.8
Botswana	34	0.3	–		362	0.0
Burkina Faso	39	0.6	56	0.8	580	0.2
Burundi	20.2		12	0.3	308	0.8
Cameroon	12.1		25	0.6	775	0.9
Cape Verde	3.5		–		166	0.3
Central African Republic	–		–		139	0.4
Chad	2.4		37	0.5	394	0.7
Comoros	–		–		64	0.7
Congo, Democratic Republic	55	0.2	87	0.5	1,207	0.6
Congo, Republic	7	0.0	–		286	0.0
Côte d'Ivoire	–		–		1,143	0.5
Djibouti	5	0.3	0	0.3	114	0.2
Egypt	–		284	0.3	2,013	0.8
Equatorial Guinea	–		–		67	0.2
Eritrea	18	0.6	–		78	0.8
Ethiopia	62	0.0	43	0.6	1,463	0.1
Gabon	76	0.3	15	0.4	688	0.8
Gambia	5	0.0	5	0.5	220	0.6
Ghana	12	0.8	86	0.0	954	0.6
Guinea	–		22	0.7	563	0.2
Guinea-Bissau	–		1	0.4	179	0.1
Kenya	51	0.3	41	0.5	724	0.2
Lesotho	0	0.8	–		300	0.6
Liberia	–		–		154	0.0
Libya	–		–		–	
Madagascar	45	0.2	57	0.3	577	0.6
Malawi	12	0.0	15	0.4	606	0.0
Mali	33	0.9	49	0.9	634	0.5
Mauritania	7	0.0	0	0.3	351	0.5
Mauritius	–		7	0.7	279	0.3
Morocco	369	0.3	175	0.7	3,891	0.1
Mozambique	30	0.0	9	0.5	915	0.1
Namibia	59	0.1	–		167	0.8
Niger	3	0.0	40	0.7	342	0.4
Nigeria	1	0.7	108	0.3	2,306	0.4
Rwanda	51	0.9	–		411	0.2
São Tomé and Príncipe	–		–		99	0.6
Senegal	9	0.6	83	0.2	669	0.5
Seychelles	–		0	0.3	89	0.8
Sierra Leone	3	0.6	39	0.7	279	0.2
Somalia	–		0	0.3	151	0.1

(Table continued on next page)

Table A2.2 (continued)

Country	2004		2005		Cumulative total*	
South Africa	117	0.1	–		511	0.0
Sudan	–		–		350	0.9
Swaziland	–		0	0.4	294	0.6
Tanzania	114	0.7			924	0.7
Togo	–		–		185	0.2
Tunisia	140	0.2	181	0.7	3,501	0.8
Uganda	74	0.2	88	0.5	944	0.4
Zambia	13	0.7	0	0.4	658	0.0
Zimbabwe	–		0	0.4	726	0.9
Multinational	219	0.2	85	0.8	1,151	0.9
Total	1,733	0.1	1,742	0.9	36,691	0.2

Source: *Annual Report 2005*, www.afdb.org

Note:
* Since the initial operation of the three institutions (1967 for ADB, 1974 for ADF and 1976 for NTF).

ADB eligible borrowers

Interventions eligible countries

ADB	14
ADF	39
ADB and ADF	2
NTF	All regional countries

African Development Bank (hard window) countries

Algeria	Gabon
Botswana	Mauritius
Egypt	Morocco
Equatorial Guinea	Namibia
Nigeria*	Swaziland
Seychelles	Tunisia
South Africa	Zimbabwe*

African Development Fund (soft window) countries

Angola	Lesotho
Benin	Liberia
Burkina Faso	Madagascar
Burundi	Malawi
Cameroon	Mali
Cape Verde	Mauritania
Central African Rep.	Mozambique
Chad	Niger
Comoros	Nigeria*
Congo, Dem. Rep.	Rwanda
Congo, Rep.	Sao Tome and Principe
Côte d'Ivoire	Senegal
Djibouti	Sierra Leone
Eritrea	Somalia
Ethiopia	Sudan
Gambia	Tanzania
Ghana	Togo
Guinea	Uganda
Guinea-Bissau	Zambia
Kenya	Zimbabwe*

Notes:
* Nigeria and Zimbabwe are eligible for both facilities.
Libya is a member but is not eligible for borrowing.

Appendix 3
Directory of African economic institutions

The United Nations Economic Commission on Africa (ECA)

The organization was created by the Economic and Social Council of the United Nations in 1958 to promote economic and social development in Africa. The website is maintained in English and French.

Menelik II Avenue
P.O. Box 3001, Addis Ababa, Ethiopia
Tel: 251-11-551-7200
Fax: 251-11-551-4416
1-212-963-4957 (New York)
www.uneca.org

The African Development Bank (ADB)

The ADB is a regional multilateral development finance institution established in 1964 and engaged in mobilizing resources toward the economic and social progress of Africa. The website is maintained in English and French.

ADB Temporary Relocation Agency (Tunis)
Angle des trois rues: Avenue du Ghana, Rue Pierre de Coubertin, Rue Hedi Nouira
B.P. 323 1002
Tunis Belvedère
Tunisia
Tel: (+216) 71-33-511/7110-3450
Fax: (+216) 71-351-933

Permanent Headquarters
Rue Joseph Anoma
01 B.P. 1387 Abidjan 01
Côte d'Ivoire
Tel: (+225) 20-20-44-44
Fax: (+225) 20-20-49-59
www.afdb.org

The New Partnership for Africa's Development (NEPAD)

The New Partnership for Africa's Development is a vision and strategic framework for Africa's renewal such as ending poverty. The website is maintained in English and French.

NEPAD Secretariat
P.O. Box 1234
The Development Bank of SA
1258 Lever Road
Midrand (Johannesburg)
1685 South Africa
Telephone: 27-11-313-3716
Fax: 27-11-313-3450
www.nepad.org

Common Market for Eastern and Southern Africa (COMESA)

COMESA is an organization dedicated to promoting regional economic integration through trade and investment. The website is in English and French.

The COMESA Centre
Ben Bella Road
P.O. Box 30051, Lusaka
Zambia
Telephone: (260-1) 229-725
Fax: (260-1) 225-107
www.comesa.int

The Community of Sahel-Saharan States (CEN-SAD)

CEN-SAD was established on 4 February 1998 to foster economic cooperation among its members. The website is in Arabic, English, and French.

CEN-SAD General Secretariat
Aljazeera Square
P.O. Box 4041
Tripoli
Telephone: (00218) 21-333-23-47; (00218) 21-333-68-03
Fax (00218) 21-444-0076
www.cen-sad.org

East African Community (EAC)

The East African Community (EAC) is the regional intergovernmental organization of the Republics of Kenya, Uganda, United Republic of Tanzania, Republic of Burundi and Republic of Rwanda. The EAC aims at cooperation among the partner states in, among others, political, economic, and social fields for their mutual benefit. The website is in English

P.O. Box 1096
Arusha
Tanzania
Telephone: 255-27-2504253/4/6/7/ 8
Fax: 255-27-2504255/2504481
www.eac.int

Economic Community of Central African States (ECCAS)

ECCAS began functioning in 1985, and aims to "achieve collective autonomy, raise the standard of living of its populations and maintain economic stability through harmonious cooperation." The website is in French, but also maintained in English, Portuguese, and Spanish.

BP. 2112 Libreville
Gabon
Telephone: (241) 44-47-31
Fax: (241) 44-47-32
www.ceeac-eccas.org

Economic Community of West African States (ECOWAS)

The Economic Community of West African states, a regional group of 15 countries, was founded in 1975 to promote economic integration in "all fields of economic activity, particularly industry, transport, telecommunications, energy, agriculture, natural resources, commerce, monetary and financial questions, social and cultural matters." The website is in English, French, and Portuguese.

60 Yakubu Gowon Crescent
Asokoro District
Abuja
Nigeria P.M.B. 401
Telephone: (234) (9) 31-47-647-9 or 47-427-9
Fax: (234) (9) 31 43 005
www.ecowas.int

Southern African Development Community (SADC)

The Southern African Development Community was created in 1980. It was formed as a loose alliance of nine majority-ruled states in Southern Africa. Its precursor SADDC aimed to lessen economic dependence on the then apartheid South Africa. The website is maintained in English, French, and Portuguese.

Private bag 0095, Gaborone
Botswana
Telephone: 267-395-1863
Fax: 267-372-848/267-318-1070
www.sadc.int

Notes

Foreword

1 Paul Theroux, *Dark Star Safari: Overland from Cairo to Cape Town* (London: Penguin, 2003), 1.
2 See Martin Meredith, *The State of Africa: A History of Fifty Years of Independence* (London: Free Press, 2006), 1–14.
3 Ian Taylor's work is a notable exception. See Ian Taylor, *NEPAD: Towards Africa's Development or Another False Start?* (Boulder, Colo.: Lynne Rienner, 2005).
4 See Katherine Marshall, *The World Bank: From Reconstruction to Development to Equity* (London: Routledge, 2008); James Vreeland, *The International Monetary Fund: Politics of Conditional Lending* (London: Routledge, 2007); and Graham Harrison, *The World Bank and Africa: The Construction of Governance States* (London: Routledge, 2004).
5 Kwame Akonor, *Africa and IMF Conditionality* (London: Routledge, 2006).

Introduction

1 IMF, *World Economic Outlook Update*, www.imf.org/external/pubs/ft/weo/2008/update/03.
2 For very current work on UNCTAD, see Ian Taylor and Karen Smith's *United Nations Conference on Trade and Development* (London and New York: Routledge, 2007). The volume is part of Routledge's Global Institutions series. The UNCTAD report can be found at *The Least Developed Countries Report*, www.unctad.org/en/docs/ldc2008_en.pdf.
3 Marcel Alfons van Meerhaeghe, *International Economic Institutions* (Dordrecht and London: Kluwer Academic Publishers, 1998).
4 For a more up to date portrait of the BWIs, see James Raymond Vreeland's *International Monetary Fund* (London and New York: Routledge, 2007) and Katherine Marshall's *The World Bank: From Reconstruction to Development to Equity* (London and New York: Routledge, 2008). Both volumes are part of Routledge's Global Institutions series. For earlier accounts, see: Michael D. Bordo and Barry Eichengreen, eds., *A Retrospective on the Bretton Woods System: Lessons for International Monetary Reform* (Chicago: University of Chicago Press, 1993); and Robert Solomon, *The International Monetary System, 1945–1981: An Insider's View* (New York: Harper and Row, 1982).

5 Markus Jachtenfuchs, "The Governance Approach to European Integration," *Journal of Common Market Studies* 39, no. 2 (2001): 245–64.

6 "Global south" refers to the developing countries. Jacqueline Braveboy-Wagner's recent contribution to Routledge's Global Institutions series, *Institutions of the Global South* (London and New York: Routledge, 2009), provides a succinct and accessible guide to the challenges and promises facing the major global south institutions.

7 For more on UN regional commissions, see Yves Berthelot, ed., *Unity and Diversity in Development Ideas: Perspectives from the U.N. Regional Commissions* (Bloomington: Indiana University Press, 2004).

8 Jeffrey Sachs, "Sources of Slow Growth in African Economies," *Development Discussion Paper* no. 545, Harvard Institute for International Development, Cambridge, Mass., July 1996.

9 Anyang' Nyong'o, *From the Lagos Plan of Action to NEPAD: The Dilemmas of Progress in Independent Africa* (Nairobi: African Academy of Sciences, 2002).

10 Ian Taylor and Philip Nel, "Getting the Rhetoric Right, Getting the Strategy Wrong: New Africa, Globalisation and the Confines of Elite Reformism," *Third World Quarterly* 23, no. 1 (February 2002): 163–80.

11 S. A. Akintan, *The Law of International Economic Institutions in Africa* (Leyden, the Netherlands: Sijthoff, 1977), 16.

12 Steven Lukes, *Power: A Radical View* (New York: Palgrave Macmillan, 2004).

1 The history of African economic institutions and their development agenda

1 The *UN Year Book* (New York: Department of Public Information, 1951), 372.

2 Fredrick Arkhurst was the lead negotiator for the Ghana delegation because Daniel Chapman, the non-resident permanent Ghanaian representative, served also as Ghana's ambassador to Washington and so was in Washington most of the time. Much of the discussion on the formation of the ECA is based on interviews conducted with Fredrick Arkhurst between February and March 2008. Fredrick Arkhurst (Ghana), together with Mahdi Elmandjra (Morocco), Mekki Abbas (Sudan), Mengesha Kifle (Ethiopia), Adebayo Adedeji (Nigeria) and Omar Loutfi (United Arab Republic of Egypt), were the African representatives who negotiated the terms of reference of the ECA.

3 Interview with Frederick S. Arkhurst, February 2008.

4 S. A. Akintan, *The Law of International Economic Institutions in Africa* (Leyden, the Netherlands: Sijthoff, 1977), 23.

5 Interview with Frederick S. Arkhurst, February 2008.

6 Interview with Frederick S. Arkhurst, February 2008.

7 Interview with Frederick S. Arkhurst, February 2008.

8 "The Economic and Social Council shall set up commissions in economic and social fields ... and such other commissions as may be required for the performance of its functions." By virtue of this article, the ECOSOC had earlier established the following commissions for their corresponding geographical areas: the Economic Commission for Europe in 1947, the Economic Commission for Asia and the Far East in 1947, and the Economic Commission for Latin America in 1948.

9 A. H. Akiwumi, "The Economic Commission for Africa," *Journal of African Law* 16, no. 3 (1972): 254–56.

10 United Nations General Assembly, 14th Session, resolution 1466, 12 December 1959.

11 United Nations General Assembly, 14th session, resolution 1466, 12 December 1959.

12 S. A. Akintan, *The Law of International Economic Institutions in Africa* (Leyden, the Netherlands: Sijthoff, 1977), 42.

13 Economic and Social Council resolution 671A (XXX) of 29 April 1958. This was later amended by resolution 974D (XXVI) of 5 July 1963 and by resolution 1343 (XLV) of 18 July 1968.

14 Akintan, *The Law of International Economic Institutions in Africa*, 48–52.

15 The UN had in the meantime provided full endorsement of the ADB idea. ECOSOC, in its resolution 874 (XXXIII) of 13 April 1962, had affirmed the need to provide the "necessary substantive and administrative support for the purpose of establishing the Bank and expressed the hope that the General Assembly would approve the request for financial resources required to implement ECA's decision on the establishment of the Bank."

16 Philip English and Harris M. Mule, *The African Development Bank* (Boulder, Colo.: Lynne Rienner, 1991), 22.

17 Interview, *Jeune Afrique* no. 1978 (8–14 December 1998).

18 African Development Bank, *The Quest for Quality: Report of the Task Force on Project Quality* (Generally known as the Knox Report, April 1994), 5.

19 Ben Edwards, "Time to scrap the AfDB?" *Euromoney* (May 1995): 46–49.

20 "A Divided Bank," *Economist* (8 July 1995): 72.

21 Paragraph 8 (iv) of the 9 September 1999 OAU Sirte Declaration mandated "Current Chairman, President Abdelaziz Bouteflika of Algeria, and President Thabo Mbeki of South Africa, to engage African creditors on our behalf on the issue of Africa's external indebtedness, with a view to securing the total cancellation of Africa's debt, as a matter of urgency."

22 Founded in April 1955, the NAM aims to represent the interests of its 118 developing country members by not aligning with any major power bloc. The Group of 77 (G-77) was established on 15 June 1964 by 77 developing countries that signed a joint declaration at the end of the first session of the United Nations Conference on Trade and Development (UNCTAD) in Geneva. The group exists to articulate and promote the collective economic interests of the global south. There are currently 130 members. For more on global south institutions, see Jacqueline Braveboy-Wagner's recent contribution to Routledge's Global Institutions series, *Institutions of the Global South* (London: Routledge, 2009).

23 While the OAU Lomé Declaration (12 July 2000) made no mention of the need for an African development document, it referenced the need for the OAU leadership to "reinvigorate the OAU Contact Group on Africa's External Debt."

24 The mandate to articulate a Compact emanated from the eighth session of the conference of African ministers of finance held from 21 to 22 November 2000. The Compact had similar objectives as MAP, and was ECA's response to the adoption of the UN Millennium Development Goals.

25 For more on this history, see Thandika Mkandawire and Charles C. Soludo, *Our Continent, Our Future: African Perspectives on Structural*

Adjustment (Dakar, Senegal: CODESRIA; Trenton, N.J.: Africa World Press, 1999).

26 Mkandawire and Soludo, *Our Continent, Our Future: African Perspectives on Structural Adjustment.*

27 Paul Collier and Jan Gunning "Explaining African Economic Performance," *Journal of Economic Literature* XXXVII (March 1999): 64–111.

28 Mkandawire and Soludo, *Our Continent, Our Future*, 25.

29 The IMF acknowledges that between 1980 and 1990, as many as half of their Africa programs were not working. Similarly, the World Bank admits that two-thirds of its programs in Africa have failed. See John W. Harbeson and Donald Rothchild, eds., *Africa in World Politics* (Boulder, Colo.: Westview Press, 2009), 47.

30 Harbeson and Rothchild, *Africa in World Politics*, 43.

31 Adedeji Adebayo, *From the Lagos Plan of Action to the New Partnership for African Development and from the Final Act of Lagos to the Constitutive Act: Whither Africa?* A Keynote address to the African Forum for envisioning Africa, 26 – 29 April 2002, Nairobi, Kenya. (available online at: www.worldsummit2002.org/texts/AdebayoAdedeji2.pdf 2002).

32 Adebayo, *From the Lagos Plan of Action to the New Partnership for African Development and from the Final Act of Lagos to the Constitutive Act: Whither Africa?*, para. 12.

33 World Bank, *Accelerated Development for Africa: an Agenda for Africa* (Washington, DC: World Bank, 1981), 3.

34 World Bank, *Adjustment in Africa: Reforms, Results and the Road Ahead* (Washington, DC: World Bank, 1994), 61.

35 For a good summary and critique of the LPA/Berg Report debate, see John Ravenhill, ed., *Africa in Economic Crisis* (Basingstoke: Macmillan, 1986).

36 Mkandiwire and Solubo, *Our Continent, Our Future*, 3.

37 Reginald Herbold Green, "The IMF and the World Bank in Africa: How Much Learning?" in *Hemmed In: Responses to Africa's Economic Decline*, ed. Thomas M. Callaghy and John Ravenhill (New York: Columbia University Press, 1993), 68.

38 Jeffery Herbst, *The Politics of Reform in Ghana 1982–1991* (Berkeley: University of California Press, 1993), 142.

39 Organization of African Unity, *Africa's Submission to the Special Session of the United Nations General Assembly on Africa's Economic and Social Crisis* (Addis Ababa: OAU, 1986).

40 Interview with Ambassador Arkhurst, February 2008.

41 English and Mule, *African Development Bank*, 63.

42 African Development Bank, "The Contribution of African Development Bank to Economic Knowledge and Policy in Africa," *Economic Research Papers* no. 58 (2000): 7.

43 Karen Mingst, *Politics and the African Development Bank* (Lexington, Ky.: University Press of Kentucky, 1990).

44 African Development Bank, "The Contribution of African Development Bank to Economic Knowledge and Policy in Africa," 19.

45 Center for Global Development, "Building Africa's Development Bank: Six Recommendations for the AfDB and its Shareholders," August 2006, 9. Washington, DC: Center for Global Development.

46 English and Mule, *African Development Bank*, 78.

47 English and Mule, *African Development Bank*, 80.
48 English and Mule, *African Development Bank*, 5.
49 Too numerous to list; for a comprehensive critique see Patrick Bond, ed., *Fanon's Warning: A Civil Society Reader on the New Partnership for African Development* (Trenton, N.J.: Africa World Press, 2002).
50 R. Gibb, T. Hughes, G. Mills, and T. Vaahtoranta, eds., *Charting a New Course: Globalisation, African Recovery and the New Africa Initiative* (Johannesburg, South Africa: SAII, 2002); and Peter Anyang' Nyong'o, Aseghedech Ghirmazion, and Davinder Lamba, eds., *NEPAD: A New Path?* (Nairobi, Kenya: Heinrich Böll Foundation, 2001).
51 Jimi O. Adesina, Yao Graham, and Adebayo O. Olukoshi, eds., *Africa and Development Challenges in the New Millennium: The NEPAD Debate* (London: Zed Books, 2006), 6.
52 Adesina, Graham, and Olukoshi, *Africa and Development Challenges in the New Millennium*, 276.
53 Francis Fukuyama, "The End of History?" in *The National Interest* (Summer 1989): 4. See also his *The End of History and the Last Man* (New York: Free Press, 1992).

2 Structure and activities of the African IEOs

1 S. A. Akintan, *The Law of International Economic Institutions in Africa* (Leyden, the Netherlands: Sijthoff, 1977), 39.
2 United Nations, Economic Commission for Africa, *ECA Business Plan— 2007–2009* (Addis Ababa, Ethiopia: Economic Commission for Africa, 2006), 26.
3 The ECA was very instrumental in convening the First World Conference on Women, in Mexico in 1975, which led to the creation of the United Nations Development Fund for Women (UNIFEM).
4 United Nations, Economic Commission for Africa, *ECA Business Plan— 2007–2009* (Addis Ababa, Ethiopia: Economic Commission for Africa, 2006), 26.
5 As of July 2008 a new CEO was being sought.
6 NEPAD, *NEPAD Dialogue*, NEPAD secretariat, South Africa, 25 January 2008, 2.

3 Toward a heterodox approach

1 By no means a single school or unitary approach, heterodox economics has come to designate the schools of economic thought that are considered outside of mainstream or orthodox economics.
2 Adebayo Adedeji, "Keynote Address: From the Lagos Plan Of Action to the New Partnership For African Development and from The Final Act of Lagos to the Constitutive Act: Whither Africa?" *Heinrich Böll Foundation African Forum for Envisioning Africa* (Nairobi: Heinrich Böll Foundation, 2002), 1–17.
3 A. H. Akiwumi, "The Economic Commission for Africa," *Journal of African Law* 16, no. 3 (1972): 254–56.
4 The Oral History Interview of Adebayo Adedeji, (6–7 March 2001), in *The Complete Oral History Transcripts from UN Voices*, CD-ROM (New York: United Nations Intellectual History Project, 2007), 95.

5 Yves Berthelot, *Unity and Diversity in Development Ideas: Perspectives from the UN Regional Commissions* (Bloomington: Indiana University Press, 2004), xii

6 See OECD, *Economic Survey of Africa* (Paris: OECD Publishing, 2004).

7 Philip English and Harris M. Mule, *The African Development Bank* (Boulder, Colo.: Lynne Rienner, 1991), 80.

8 English and Mule, *African Development Bank,* 43.

9 K. A. Mingst, *Politics of the African Development Bank* (Lexington, Ky.: University Press of Kentucky, 1990), 106.

10 Mingst, *Politics of the African Development Bank*, 106.

11 African Development Bank, "Stepping up to the Future: An Independent Evaluation of ADF-VII, VIII and IX," Operations Evaluation Department, ADB, Tunis, 6 August 2004.

12 Lokongo Bafalikike, "Jammeh: 'Nepad Will Never Work,'" *New African* 410 (September 2002): 18–20.

13 Pete Ondeng, "Poor Leadership Sinks NEPAD," *The Weekender* (South Africa), 23 June 2007, 8.

14 Jimi O. Adesina, Yao Graham, and Adebayo O. Olukoshi, eds., *Africa and Development Challenges in the New Millennium: The NEPAD Debate* (London: Zed Books, 2006) 90.

15 See Ha-Joon Chang, *Bad Samaritans: The Myth of Free Trade and the Secret History of Capitalism* (London: Bloomsbury Press, 2007); and Ha-Joon Chang, *Kicking Away the Ladder: Development Strategy in Historical Perspective* (London: Anthem Press, 2002).

16 Though they did not serve longer periods, Yves Berthelot notes that the ECA's first two executive secretaries, Mekki Abbas and Robert Gardiner, were not very effective since they were sent to Congo as the special representatives of the UN secretary-general. See Berthelot, *Unity and Diversity in Development Ideas*, 2.

17 See Stanley Please and K. Y. Amoako, "The World Bank's Report on Accelerated Development in Sub-Saharan Africa: A Critique of Some of the Criticism," *African Studies Review* 27, no. 4 (1984): 47–58; and also Stanley Please and K. Y. Amoako, "OAU, ECA and the World Bank: Do They Really Disagree?" in John Ravenhill, ed., *Africa in Economic Crisis* (Basingstoke: Macmillan, 1986), 127–48.

18 The Oral History Interview of Adebayo Adedeji, (6–7 March 2001), 95, in *The Complete Oral History Transcripts from UN Voices*, CD-ROM (New York: United Nations Intellectual History Project, 2007), 95.

19 Jimi Adesina, "NEPAD and the Challenge of Africa's Development: Towards the Political Economy of a Discourse," unpublished paper, Department of Sociology, Rhodes University, Grahamstown, 2002.

20 Ian Taylor and Philip Nel, "Getting the Rhetoric Right, Getting the Strategy Wrong: 'New Africa,' Globalisation and the Confines of Elite Reformism," *Third World Quarterly* 23, no.1 (February 2002): 163–80.

21 Berthelot, *Unity and Diversity in Development Ideas*, 245.

22 Berthelot, *Unity and Diversity in Development Ideas*, 269.

23 Analysis on African development (and that of the global south) can be broadly viewed through two lenses: the liberal and the critical tradition. Though there are variants and revisions within each perspective, the liberal tradition usually assumes that for Africa to develop it would have to imitate

the values and institutions of its Western counterparts. The critical tradition on hand rejects this linear path-dependence and argues that African development rests on breaking free from its structural and cultural dependence on Western institutions, and replacing them with endogenous policies. For more on this, see Peter Schraeder, *African Politics and Society: A Mosaic in Transformation* (Belmont, Calif.: Wadsworth, 2004), 301–37.

24 Frantz Fanon, *The Wretched of the Earth* (trans. C. Farrington, New York: Grove Press, 1963), 52.

25 Neocolonialism refers to a condition in which, despite political independence, a newly independent state remains vulnerable and sensitive to external manipulation due to the continuing control of its economy by colonial and imperial powers. See Kwame Nkrumah, *Africa Must Unite* (New York: International Publishers, 1970).

26 The Oral History Interview of Adebayo Adedeji (6–7 March 2001), in *The Complete Oral History Transcripts from UN Voices*, CD-ROM (New York: United Nations Intellectual History Project, 2007), 57–58.

27 The failings of the neoliberal doctrines in Africa have led some to argue that the search for a developmental state should be at the forefront of a new developmental agenda in Africa. See Jamee Moudud and Karl Botchway, "Challenging the Orthodoxy: African Development in the Age of Openness," *African and Asian Studies* 6, no.4 (2007): 457–93.

28 See Ha-Joon Chang, Bad *Samaritans: The Myth of Free Trade and the Secret History of Capitalism* (London, Bloomsbury Press, 2007); and Ha-Joon Chang, *Kicking Away the Ladder: Development Strategy in Historical Perspective* (London: Anthem Press, 2002). For another take, see Alice Amsden, *Asia's Next Giant: South Korea and Late Industrialization* (Oxford: Oxford University Press, 1989).

29 The Oral History Interview of Adebayo Adedeji (6–7 March 2001), in *The Complete Oral History Transcripts from UN Voices*, CD-ROM (New York: United Nations Intellectual History Project, 2007), 95.

30 Kevin Gallagher, ed., *Putting Development First: The Importance of Policy Space in the WTO and IFIs* (London: Zed Books, 2005).

31 For a critique on foreign aid to Africa and how it constrains Africa's development policy choices, see Kwame Akonor, "Foreign Aid to Africa: A Hollow Hope?" *New York University Journal of International Law and Politics* 40, no. 4 (2008): 1071–78.

32 According to Dr. William Easterly, the West spent $568 billion on foreign aid to Africa between 1960 and 2000. William Easterly, "Can Foreign Aid Save Africa?" Address at the Clemens Lecture Series of Saint Johns University (December 2005), available at www.csbsju.edu/clemens/images/Clemens2005.pdf.

33 Martin Meredith, *The Fate of Africa: From the Hopes of Freedom to the Heart of Despair* (New York: Public Affairs, 2005), 683.

34 Interview with author, Fred Arkhurst, March 2008.

35 The Oral History Interview of Adebayo Adedeji (6–7 March 2001), in *The Complete Oral History Transcripts from UN Voices*, CD-ROM (New York: United Nations Intellectual History Project, 2007), 53.

36 William Easterly, "The Ideology of Development," *Foreign Policy* no. 161 (July/August 2007): 31–35.

37 Fanon, *The Wretched of the Earth*.

4 African regional economic communities

1 Margaret C. Lee, *The Political Economy of Regionalism in Southern Africa* (Cape Town, South Africa and Boulder, Colo.: UCT Press and Lynne Rienner Publishers, 2003), 8.
2 Adebayo Adedeji, Statement at the opening of the 5th Meeting of the Conference of Ministers in Rabat, 20 March 1979, UNECA, Addis Ababa, 1979.
3 See generally, M. Lakshman Marasinghe, "A Review of Regional Economic Integration in Africa with Particular Reference to Equatorial Africa," *International and Comparative Law Quarterly* 33, no.1 (1984): 39–56.
4 Adebayo Adedeji, Statement at the opening of the 5th Meeting of the Conference of Ministers in Rabat, 20 March, 1979, UNECA, Addis Ababa, 1979.
5 The idea for an African Economic Community was part of the Lagos Plan of Action (see Chapter 1).
6 See M. L. Marasinghe, "A Review of Regional Economic Integration in Africa with Particular Reference to Equatorial Africa," *International and Comparative Law Quarterly* 33, no. 1 (1984): 39–56.
7 Tom Soper, "The EEC and Aid to Africa," *International Affairs* 41, no. 3 (July 1965): 463–77.
8 For useful historical analysis on the early relationship between the EEC and African countries, see: I. W. Zartman, *The Politics of Trade Negotiations between Africa and the European Economic Community: the Weak Confront the Strong* (Princeton, N.J.: Princeton University Press, 1971).
9 For a general analysis: K. R. Simmonds, "The Lomé Convention: Implementation and Renegotiation," *Common Market Law Review* 16, no. 3 (1979): 425.
10 The Cotonou Agreement is a treaty between the European Union and the group of African, Caribbean and Pacific states (ACP countries). It was signed in June 2000 in Cotonou, the largest city in Benin, by 79 ACP countries and the then 15 member states of the European Union. It entered into force in 2003 and is the latest agreement in the history of ACP-EU Development Cooperation.
11 EU Council Statement on Development Cooperation, 1997.
12 The Treaty Establishing the Economic Community of West African States. Done at Lagos, Nigeria on 28 May 1975. Hereinafter, "1975 ECOWAS Treaty."
13 Cited in Daniel C. Bach "L'Integration economique regionale en Afrique," *Economique Perspective Internationale* 48 (4e trimester, 1991): 37.
14 The EBID was created as the financial arm of ECOWAS in December 1999, replacing the ECOWAS Fund for Cooperation, Compensation and Development.
15 See Article 6 of the Treaty Establishing the Economic Community of Central African States for the procedures for establishing the Community.
16 South Africa or SADCC, Not Both," *Economist*, 22 January 1983, 60.
17 Article 5, SADC Treaty (1992).
18 Seychelles was readmitted to SADC in August 2007.
19 Zahira Kharsany, "Ground-breaking Gender Protocol Signed," *Inter Press Service News Agency*, 18 August 2008, http://ipsnews.net/africa/nota.asp?idnews=43593.

20 United Nations, Economic Commission for Africa, *Assessing Regional Integration in Africa: Rationalizing Regional Economic Communities* (Addis Ababa, Ethiopia: Economic Commission for Africa, 2006), 52.

21 United Nations, Economic Commission for Africa, *Assessing Regional Integration in Africa* (ECA Policy Research Report, 2004), 41.

22 Economic Commission for Africa, *Assessing Regional Integration in Africa*, 41.

23 Economic Commission for Africa, *Assessing Regional Integration in Africa*, 7.

24 CTA Economic and Export Analysts Ltd., *The ECOWAS Trade Liberalisation Scheme, Draft Study Report for the Ministry of Trade and Tourism of Ghana* (London: CTA, 1992), 14.

25 For a good review of this literature see, Ousmane Badiane, "National Policies as Impediments to Regional Economic Integration," in *Regional Integration and Co-operation in West Africa: A Multidimensional Perspective*, ed. Réal Lavergne (Trenton, N.J.: Africa World Press and Ottawa: IDRC, 1997), chapter 8; and Timothy Shaw, "Regionalism and the African Crisis: Towards a Political Economy of ECOWAS and SADCC," in *West African Regional Co-operation and Development*, ed. Julius Emeka Okolo and Stephen Wright (Boulder, Colo.: Westview Press, 1990), 115–145.

26 Ominiyi Adewoye, "Constitutionalism and and Economic Integration," in Lavergne, *Regional Integration and Cooperation in West Africa: A Multidimensional Perspective*, 328–29.

27 Donald L. Sparks, "Economic Trends in Africa South of the Sahara," *Europa World Online*, www.europaworld.com/entry/ass.essay.2.

28 ILO (International Labor Organization) "HIV/AIDS: A Threat to Decent Work, Productivity and Development," Document for discussion at the Special High-Level Meeting on HIV/AIDS and the World of Work, 8 June 2000, Geneva.

29 Samuel Crowe and Ike Anya, "Health and Medical Issues in Sub-Saharan Africa," *Europa World Online*, www.europaworld.com/entry/ass.essay.3.

30 See OAU, *Protocol on Relations between the African Economic Community and the Regional Economic Communities* (February 1998), www.iss.co.za/AF/RegOrg/unity_to_union/pdfs/aec/recprotocol.pdf.

31 The Club du Sahel was formed in 1976 to bring together the Sahelian states belonging to the Permanent Inter-State Committee for the Prevention of Drought in the Sahel (CILSS). Its membership includes nation states such as Burkina Faso, Cape Verde, Chad, the Gambia, Guinea-Bissau, Mali, Mauritania, Niger, and Senegal, as well as non-government organizations. The Club is run by a secretariat based at OECD in Paris.

32 Club du Sahel, "Reforming West Africa's Intergovernmental Organisations," document prepared for the meeting of the Ministerial Lobby Group in Paris, 2–3 October 2000, SAH/GMAP(2000) 12, Club du Sahel (Paris: OECD, 2000).

33 World Bank, *World Development Indicators* (Washington, DC: World Bank, 2001), iv.

34 World Bank, *World Development Indicators*.

35 Adebayo Adedeji, "History and Prospects For Regional Integration in Africa", presented at the third meeting of the ECA's African Development Forum, Addis Ababa, 5 March 2002.

36 United Nations, Economic Commission for Africa, *Assessing Regional Integration in Africa*, 60.

37 See Peter Lloyd, "New Bilateralism in the Asia-Pacific," *The World Economy* 25, no. 9 (2002): 1279–96.
38 Reginald Herbold Green and Ann Willcox Seidman, *Unity or Poverty? The Economics of PanAfricanism* (Harmondsworth: Penguin African Library, 1968), 22.
39 Kwame Nkrumah, *Handbook of Revolutionary Warfare: A Guide to the Armed Phase of the African Revolution* (New York: International Publishers, 1969), 101.

5 Emerging issues and future direction

1 World Bank, *World Development Indicators* (Washington, DC: World Bank, 2007).
2 ECA, *The ECA 2008 Economic Report on Africa* (Addis Ababa, Ethiopia: Economic Commission for Africa, 2008), 179.
3 Michael Jennings, "A Century of Development: Policy and Process in Sub-Saharan Africa, 2007," *Europa World Online*. Retrieved 17 June 2008 from www.europaworld.com/entry/ass.essay.7.
4 For more on The MDG Africa Steering Group, see www.mdgafrica.org.
5 "United Nations to Support African Union/NEPAD Platform on eve of G-8 Meeting," United Nations Fund for International Partnerships, press release AFR/1160/DEV/2509/ECO/84), 16 May 2005.
6 Kofi Annan, "Secretary-General Cites 'Symbiotic Relationship' between Global Goals on Poverty, New Plan for Africa's Development, in Statement to General Assembly," *Africa Recovery* 16, no. 4 (February 2003): 6.
7 The other five development agencies are: the Asian Development Bank, U.K. Department for International Development (DFID), Japan Bank for International Cooperation (JBIC), KfW Entwicklungsbank (KfW development bank), and the World Bank.
8 African Development Bank, Statement on World AIDS Day, "Accountability—Ensuring Effectiveness of Our Collective Actions," 1 December 2006.
9 ECA, *The ECA 2008 Economic Report on Africa* (Addis Ababa, Ethiopia: Economic Commission for Africa, 2008), 183.
10 Jeffrey D. Sachs, John W. McArthur, Guido Schmidt Traub, Margaret Kruk, Chandrika Bahadur, Michael Faye, and Gordon McCord, "Ending Africa's Poverty Trap," Brookings Papers on Economic Activity, August 2004 (Washington, DC: Brookings Institution Press, 2004).
11 ECA, *Survey on the Monterrey Consensus* (Addis Ababa, Ethiopia: Economic Commission for Africa, March/ April 2007).
12 See John Githongo, "Corruption is the Bane of African Countries," *East African Standard*, 15 April 2005.
13 The global concern for corruption is aptly captured in the UN General Assembly's resolution 58/4 (adopted on 31 October 2003) in which it declared the 9th of December every year as "International Anti-Corruption Day."
14 Martin Meredith, *The Fate of Africa: From the Hopes of Freedom to the Heart of Despair* (New York: Public Affairs, 2005), 687. Also, Elizabeth Blunt, "Corruption Costs Africa Billions," *BBC News*, 18 September 2002, http://news.bbc.co.uk/2/hi/africa/2265387.stm.
15 Statement issued at the end of the international conference on "Institutions, Culture and Corruption in Africa" jointly organized by the ECA and the

Council for the Development of Social Science Research in Africa (CODESRIA), in Addis Ababa, 13–15 October 2008.

16 ADB, *Combating Corruption*, Conference Proceedings, Addis Ababa, 27–30 January 2003.

17 See NEPAD document, "Summary of NEPAD Action Plans," para. 8, at www.nepad.org/2005/files/documets/41.pdf.

18 For very useful analysis of the AU and NEPAD's work on corruption, see Samuel Makinda and Wafula Okumu, *The African Union: Challenges Of Globalization, Security, and Governance* (London and New York: Routledge, 2008), 58–74.

19 Makinda and Okumu, *The African Union*, 17.

20 Makinda and Okumu, *The African Union*, 70.

21 World Economic Forum on Africa 2006, *Going for Growth*, 31 May–2 June 2006 (Cape Town, South Africa).

22 As of this writing the move to consolidate NEPAD with AU had not occurred.

23 Jimi O. Adesina, Yao Graham, and Adebayo O. Olukoshi, eds., *Africa and Development Challenges in the New Millennium: The NEPAD Debate* (London: Zed Books, 2006), 7.

24 Adesina et al., *Africa and Development Challenges in the New Millennium*, 94.

25 Kwame Nkrumah, speech at launch of the OAU, Addis Abba, Ethiopia, 1963.

Select bibliography

Jimi O. Adesina, Yao Graham, and Adebayo O. Olukoshi, eds., *Africa and Development Challenges in the New Millennium: The NEPAD Debate* (London: Zed Books, 2006). Contributors to this volume examine NEPAD in relation to crosscutting issues on African development such as poverty, gender, technology, and regional development.

Patrick Bond, ed., *Fanon's Warning: A Civil Society Reader on the New Partnership for African Development* (Trenton, N.J.: Africa World Press, 2002). An annotated critique of NEPAD that investigates whether Africa's new development blueprint is another extension of neocolonial globalization. Its main point of reference is a critical examination of African governing elites and their partnerships "with the decadence of the bourgeoisie of the West," a phenomenon Frantz Fanon elaborated on in his book, *The Wretched of the Earth*.

Eric Edi, *Globalization and Politics in the Economic Community of West African States* (Durham, N.C.: Carolina Academic Press, 2007). This book discusses the history and achievements of ECOWAS as well as the political and economic consequences of globalization on the institution.

E. Philip English and Harris M. Mule, *The African Development Bank* (Boulder, Colo.: Lynne Rienner, 1996). Provides an in-depth look at the policies and projects of the African Development Bank and makes recommendations and suggestions on how to strengthen the institution.

J. Andrew Grant and Fredrik Söderbaum, *The New Regionalism in Africa* (Aldershot: Ashgate, 2003). A good treatise on regionalism theories and their empirical import on security and development dynamics for Africa.

Francis Nguendi Ikome, *From the Lagos Plan of Action to the New Partnership for Africa's Development* (Midrand, South Africa: Institute for Global Dialogue, 2007). A valuable contribution to understanding the inward-looking strategy of "collective self-reliance" espoused by the LPA and the political and economic reform agenda advocated by NEPAD.

Samuel Makinda and Wafula Okumu, *The African Union: Challenges of Globalization, Security, and Governance* (London and New York: Routledge, 2008). A critical look at Africa's premier political institution, the Organization of African Unity (OAU) and its evolution into the African Union (AU).

Challenges to the AU such as human rights, governance, and security issues are analyzed in a balanced manner.

Bade Onimode, *African Development and Governance Strategies in the 21st Century* (London and New York: Zed Books, 2004). This is a collection of essays written by African scholars in honor of Professor Adebayo Adedeji's 70th birthday. It discusses development challenges confronting the continent and offers alternative paradigms.

Ian Taylor, *NEPAD: Towards Africa's Development or Another False Start?* (Boulder, Colo.: Lynne Rienner, 2005). Argues that NEPAD is not transformative and like previous development models lacks popular legitimacy.

United Nations, Economic Commission for Africa, *Assessing Regional Integration in Africa: Rationalizing Regional Economic Communities* (Addis Ababa, Ethiopia: Economic Commission for Africa, 2006). This policy research report produced by the ECA reflects on the integration schemes on the continent and argues for the need to rationalize the numerous Regional Economic Communities.

Index

Note: Page numbers in **bold** indicate tables and figures.

GLOBAL INSTITUTIONS SERIES

NEW TITLE
Global Institutions and the HIV/AIDS Epidemic
Responding to an international crisis

Franklyn Lisk, University of Warwick, UK

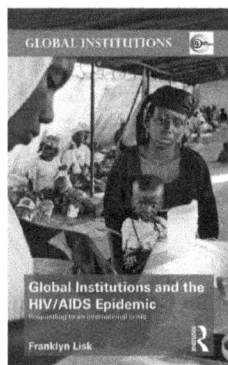

Lisk examines the different perspectives of the global response to HIV/AIDS and the role of the different global institutions (multilateral, public and private) involved, including their impact on outcomes.

Selected contents: 1 The evolution HIV/AIDS as a global epidemic and early global response 2 The rise and fall of the global programme on AIDS (GPA) 3 The birth of the joint United Nations programme on HIV/AIDS (UNAIDS) 4 HIV/AIDS and human rights 5 HIV/AIDS as a security threat 6 HIV/AIDS as a development challenge 7 HIV/AIDS and human resource capacity 8 Financing of the global HIV/AIDS response 9 Global governance and HIV/AIDS response 10 Critical and emerging issues and challenges in HIV/AIDS response

September 2009: 216x138: 160pp
Hb: 978-0-415-44496-5: **£65.00**
Pb: 978-0-415-44497-2: **£14.99**

NEW TITLE
Regional Security
The capacity of international organizations

Rodrigo Tavares, United Nations University

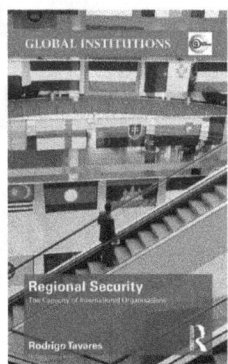

This book is the first systematic study of the capacities of the most recognized intergovernmental organizations with a security mandate.

Selected contents: 1 International organizations in regional security 2 African Union (AU) 3 Economic Community of West African States (ECOWAS) 4 Intergovernmental Authority on Development (IGAD) 5 Southern African Development Community (SADC) 6 Organization of American States (OAS) 7 Association of Southeast Asian Nations (ASEAN) 8 Commonwealth of Independent States (CIS) 9 League of Arab States (LAS) 10 Pacific Islands Forum (PIF) 11 European Union (EU) 12 North Atlantic Treaty Organization (NATO)

July 2009: 216x138: 232pp
Hb: 978-0-415-48340-7: **£75.00**
Pb: 978-0-415-48341-4: **£16.99**

Routledge
Taylor & Francis Group

To order any of these titles
Call: +44 (0) 1235 400400
Email: book.orders@routledge.co.uk

For further information visit:
www.routledge.com/politics

eBooks – at www.eBookstore.tandf.co.uk

A library at your fingertips!

eBooks are electronic versions of printed books. You can store them on your PC/laptop or browse them online.

They have advantages for anyone needing rapid access to a wide variety of published, copyright information.

eBooks can help your research by enabling you to bookmark chapters, annotate text and use instant searches to find specific words or phrases. Several eBook files would fit on even a small laptop or PDA.

NEW: Save money by eSubscribing: cheap, online access to any eBook for as long as you need it.

Annual subscription packages

We now offer special low-cost bulk subscriptions to packages of eBooks in certain subject areas. These are available to libraries or to individuals.

For more information please contact webmaster.ebooks@tandf.co.uk

We're continually developing the eBook concept, so keep up to date by visiting the website.

www.eBookstore.tandf.co.uk

For Product Safety Concerns and Information please contact our EU
representative GPSR@taylorandfrancis.com
Taylor & Francis Verlag GmbH, Kaufingerstraße 24, 80331 München, Germany